THE ORNAMENTAL HERMIT

THE ORNAMENTAL

HERMIT

People and Places of the New West

ROBERT MURRAY DAVIS

TEXAS TECH UNIVERSITY PRESS

This book is typeset in Scala. The paper used in this book meets the
minimum requirements of ANSI/NISO Z39.48-1992 (R1997). ∞

Designed by Jeff LeJune

Printed in the United States of America

Library of Congress Cataloging-in-Publication Data
Davis, Robert Murray.
The Ornamental Hermit : People and Places of the New West /
Robert Murray Davis.
p. cm.
ISBN 0-89672-523-5 (cloth : alk. paper)
1. West (U.S.)—Description and travel. 2. West (U.S.)—Social life
and customs. 3. West (U.S.)—Biography. 4. Davis, Robert Murray.
I. Title.
F595.3.D38 2004
917.8—dc22
2003024632

03 04 05 06 07 08 09 10 11 / 9 8 7 6 5 4 3 2 1

Texas Tech University Press
Box 41037
Lubbock, Texas 79409-1037 USA
800.832.4042
ttup@ttu.edu
www.ttup.ttu.edu

For Jane Lancaster and
Dave and Fran McPherson

CONTENTS

Contents

PREFACE

West is where we all plan to go some day.

All the King's Men

Most of the pieces that follow were the result of my driving across, and occasionally stopping in, the American West. For many years of college and graduate school, my intellectual and physical orientation were eastward, but only when I went all the way to Europe did I begin to realize how American, and how Western, I was and am.

Of course, I had watched two-for-a-dime Western movies at the Casino Theater in Boonville, Missouri, as a child, and even into graduate school read genre Westerns, but until the 1980s I had done little traveling in the real West, and even then mostly back and forth to the Llano Estacado for reasons that were as much personal as professional, and when I stopped going there I realized that I missed the journey as much as, perhaps more than, the person I had traveled to see.

More often, circumstances had led me eastward, to Nova Scotia and New Brunswick. Driving in the East is physically and spiritually different from driving in the West because you can't see as far or as much, even the gas stations indicated by the signboards on the interstate highways in Pennsylvania, for example, so that you never know if they are really there or how far, or which direction, you'll have to go to reach them. In contrast, and characteristically, on I-70 in Kansas a billboard advertises a business two miles ahead—and you can see the business as soon as you see the sign.

Gaston Bachelard says in *The Poetics of Space* that "All great, simple images reveal a psychic state" and that daydream "contemplates grandeur" and seeks "the space of *elsewhere*." Going into the West has restored my ability to dream, to return to imaginative states for which years of academic work had offered no outlet.

Of course, I keep being reminded that the West is a real place that no film or fiction or for that matter nonfiction can quite embody. Thus, while the movie can show landscape, it cannot—except with the most painfully obvious devices—show geography. Traveling in the real West has given me new understanding and appreciation of the landscape and the people, not just supernumeraries, as in the films, who inhabit it. Those include not just long-term residents who aren't always aware that they embody a mythos but the newcomers attracted as much by their ideas of the West as by the places themselves. There are plenty of things wrong with the West, as environmental critics and political activists will be quick to tell you, but the places and people still have unique qualities that I hope are celebrated in this collection.

These essays, written over the past decade, are attempts to pay tribute to the ideas of the West as well as to the people who came there over the past two or three centuries. They don't try very hard to separate myth from reality because the two keep blending and separating and coloring each other.

I'm particularly indebted to Jane Lancaster and David and Fran McPherson, who gave me the chance to live in New Mexico, and to Moses Glidden and Dinah Owens, who got me to Arizona. The members of the Western Literature Association have given me a new understanding not only of the writers who celebrate the region but also of the environment and its inhabitants. Jeanette Harris and Sarah Nestor read early drafts of some of these essays. The editors of the journals in which some of them first appeared gave me the chance to stretch myself and pretend long and hard enough to become, in part, at least, what I had always wanted to be.

THE ORNAMENTAL HERMIT

INTRODUCTION
One-Night Stands

If we do not find something pleasant, we
may at least find something new.

Candide

At an international conference in Maritime Canada, some of the Europeans were astonished that I had chosen to drive two thousand miles rather than fly. One said, "Isn't it terribly difficult sleeping in a different bed every night?"

"Well," I said, "it depends on how you train for it."

Some of them already seemed convinced that, what with my mid/southwest/southern/rustbelt accent, I was straight out of a Waylon Jennings song, so they may have inferred a sexual innuendo. Mostly I was referring to my travel habits, but in fact coming into a new town every night is not unlike the early stages of a potential love affair. It's possible to fall a little in love with an unfamiliar town you'll never see again.

Or at least it is for me. Perhaps this is because, as a child of the Dust Bowl Depression, I grew up traveling. Before I started kindergarten in 1939, my parents had moved from one town (and in one case a farm) to another six different times. The first move I remember, and the last one, from Arkansas City, Kansas, to Boonville, Missouri, was in a 1938 Chevrolet coupe with me lying on the flat space between the seat and the back window, sharing space with a Spitz named Cubby.

That summer I rode the train, alone (with someone paid to look after me, though I did not know it), from Sedalia, Missouri, to someplace in Kansas where I was met by my father's half-sister, who took me to Albuquerque, New Mexico, where I stayed with another aunt and her family and had a great time following my older cousin and being made welcome by that branch of the family.

Later, during World War II, I was sent, alone, on a bus from Boonville to Evansville, Indiana, to spend the summer with my maternal grandparents. Instead of going through Indianapolis on the big bus, I took a Victory Bus (red, white, and blue school bus) labeled "Evansville" and got there two hours before my grandparents expected me. Since they weren't there, I took a taxi to their house and waited on the steps until they came home. My grandmother took weeks to get over the experience, but my grandfather seemed rather pleased at my ingenuity.

This pleasure at seeing new things extends to a recurrent dream I've had over the years. In a house that seems, at least in dream, familiar, I open a door to find a whole suite of rooms, sometimes in the cellar, sometimes adjoining the main or second floor or both, and am delighted to discover new and unexpected space.

Perhaps that's why I take pleasure in moving alone through space toward a destination I've chosen. At first, when I was doing research in Austin at the University of Texas Humanities Research Center (only later the Harry H. Ransom HRC), it was a destination with a definite purpose, though I found that I enjoyed the time alone as much as I did the research and the chance to meet people from places I had never been and barely heard of and who gave me a sense of a world bigger than I imagined and in some cases the chance to go there.

But after I ended that research project and, almost coincidentally, my marriage, I began to travel with less definite purposes. Even more than the gurus claim, the journey came to matter more than the arrival. Driving across country is, for me, anyway, a kind of release. The farther I get from familiar territory—mail, bills, appointments, obligations, conflicts—the more I feel my mind letting these things ripple out into the country's emptiness and to see a whole series of patterns.

Some of these are physical patterns, like the windbreaks in Kansas, north of Wichita, that angle oddly into roads and fencerows. This implies a world made regular by human intervention, subject to man. North and west, humans have had less impact on land that is rolling, curved, punctuated lightly by trees and vegetation, almost female in contour. Or patterns conflict, like the rows of wheat leading to the walls of churches and houses no longer used by their builders. Whole towns where the world passed, looked, and walked away, like Goldfield, Utah, seat of Esmerelda County, which doesn't even get a listing in my road atlas and is lined with boarded-up buildings. The town in Oregon whose only distinction is that it lies on the 45th parallel, half-way between the North Pole and the equator. Sad desert burgs like Wittman, Arizona, littered with trash and old trailers. Near third-world towns like Chama, New Mexico, where only the nomadic Anglos in the RV park show any evidence of prosperity. Page, Arizona, created by the Glen Canyon Dam, which is not sad but, in every subtle detail, just out of place. Everywhere one can see effects, though the causes and conditions might be obscure to the casual passerby.

I've spent a good deal of time in the West, but I'm not exactly *of* the West. I grew up in Boonville, on the Missouri River. Although it still has barge traffic and now a land-locked casino boat, people there don't really see it as a thoroughfare. Instead, it is a boundary, something to be crossed. Kit Carson left for the West from Franklin, just across the river, before it was washed away. Boonville is near enough to the starting point for the Santa Fe Trail, and the street of that name is closer than usual to something more than a developer's fantasy.

Crossing the river the other way meant, to me, going east—to Columbia, the academic center of Missouri, and to St. Louis, definitely eastern and according to the natives the intellectual capital of the state and perhaps the world. In the other direction, Kansas City was disquietingly large and unfamiliar, but it was not, like St. Louis, alien.

Of course, the people I saw, even the ones who owned horses, weren't cowboys—they were farmers. Like many males of my generation, I thought of the West as a region that existed more in imagination or perhaps in fantasy than in anyplace on a map. I didn't want to be a farmer or a mountain man or a wagon master or a Santa Fe trader. I wanted to be a cowboy.

I never became one—dealing with horses and cattle didn't make me like them as well as I did the cinematic ones—but half a century after I left Boonville for college, I became president of the Western Literature Association at the end of a series of long and circuitous journeys.

Many of these have taken me physically through the West, where I have seen patterns that remind me of those in my own life but blessedly have no direct connection to it. Thus I can be a spectator not only of others' lives but in an important sense of my own. That sense of detachment allows me to feel a temporary sense of connection to places where I don't and never will know anyone and may speak only to check into a motel and order food.

My first experience of this sensation was on my first road trip east in 1981. I'd chosen Richmond, Indiana, because Bix Beiderbecke had recorded there, and I discovered that the edge of town, near the interstate, was convenient for the traveler, and the older part of town was clean, well laid out, and charming. A day later, in Bloomsburg, Pennsylvania, still farther from home and the problems I left, I experienced an unaccountable sense of happiness while driving through tree-lined streets that reminded me a little of the town where I grew up and which I spent my first twenty years trying to escape.

Since then, a number of towns have captured my imagination in the same way. Bluff, Utah, for its funky, river-runner culture, lovely, stark bluffs, the rustic-looking motel with books and a lecture on local ecology and a clerk who spoke scornfully of the bland Mormon town to the north. Fallon, Nevada, seemingly an oasis of green and civility after hundreds of miles of desolation on U.S. 93 up from Las Vegas, for the helpful Lithuanian motel owner, the good meal at the modest local casino—but, as I then learned, a place where children are dying of cancer at an alarming rate—the librarian who let me use her computer to check my e-mail, the quiet, pleasant streets. Nebraska City, Nebraska, founding place of Arbor Day, one of those holidays no one can remember, a Missouri River town eclipsed by Omaha that has its own character and understated energy. Baker City, Oregon, which I've never entered but which looks from the interstate nice enough to be, as advertised, the point at which emigrants on the Oregon Trail first saw that their journey might be worthwhile after all. Cole Camp, Missouri, where some of the buildings are being restored and a born-again baker has found spiritual peace and makes pretty good cinnamon rolls.

But some towns are just not likeable, just as some men and women do not seem desirable. I've tried to become interested in Las Vegas, New Mexico, which keeps promising to be the new Taos but never is. Passersby on the interstate find it difficult to enter and leave, gasoline is twenty cents a gallon higher than in Raton, and the stations are even seedier than the downtown area—where, on the plaza, the hotel clerk urges guests to park a block away in the police department lot because of break-ins—and there is no discernible street life because, one hears, of hostility between Anglos and Hispanics dating back to the Mexican War.

While I don't want to go back to Las Vegas, I wouldn't mind returning to Bluff or Nebraska City or Fallon. They are charming places—just as Boonville seems charming to my friends who have passed through. But I wouldn't want to live there. And I remember that in the dream about the undiscovered rooms, the pleasure at discovery is soon supplanted by a sense of anxiety about what I am going to *do* with all that room that is suddenly available for use.

The solution, in waking life, has been to keep moving, observing, and recording. Only recently did I discover, while watching cable in a provincial Slovenian town, the term that some might use to describe my symptoms: oikophobia, which means fear of home. The announcer added that oikophobes would rather be in a cheap hotel room than at home. I thought that this described writers, or certain kinds of writers like me or my friend Frank Chin, who, at a symposium of ethnic Chinese in Singapore on the topic "Where Is Home?" announced, "My home is my writing. My home is my craft, my art" (*Bulletproof Buddhists*).

I have a home, or several homes, besides my craft, and I don't hate them. Sometimes I want to leave, though I don't always know where I am going. If I have had a destination, I'm not always sure what I find. But that's the chief interest in going somewhere, and I think you can't really know what home is if that is the only thing you know. Everything is always compared to what, and I have sought, and enjoyed, the "what" over the past quarter century, some of it in the American West. And some not, though that is another set of stories and perhaps, as they say in Oklahoma, a whole 'nother book.

ORIGINS

THE SHORTEST WAY HOME

Buda-Pesth seems a wonderful place.
Dracula

I don't deny my name.
Jelly Roll Morton

In September, 1981, on the afternoon of my forty-seventh birthday, I leaned against the retaining wall in the courtyard of the palace on Castle Hill in Budapest and looked across the Danube at Pest, spread out as far as I could see on the great plain that ends at the Carpathians. Later it occurred to me that my situation was like that of a Henry James hero, America far behind me and a whole new world to look at. But at the time I didn't feel at all Jamesian. Instead, I was feeling very sorry for myself because I was not merely alone, which I could manage, but I didn't know a soul for thousands of miles. More daunting still, I didn't know a word of Hungarian, which, to a monoglot speaker of an Indo-European language, is as foreign as a language can get and still use the roman alphabet. Forced to rely on my inner resources, I wasn't sure I had any.

It was my third day in Budapest, and someone recovering from a first case of jet lag finds it hard to feel Jamesian or even Hemingwayesque. I had boarded a plane in the flatlands of Oklahoma, struggled through the humidity of JFK and then through the confusion of Heathrow. Suddenly the plane had dipped to an even flatter landscape than I was used to and, far from the terminal, passed over a man in uniform with a machine gun slung on his left shoulder. In the States, I had brushed off questions about going behind the Iron

Curtain with the semiofficial view that Hungary was different. But, it seemed in 1981, not all that different.

Then and later, people asked, "Why Hungary?" There was a logical though somewhat torturous explanation. I had gotten through a divorce; I was disaffected with my job. The solution, typically American, was to go somewhere else, and since I was unqualified to ship out on a whaler or sign up for a cattle drive, it was easier to become a Fulbrighter and go to Europe, where none of my family had been since my maternal great-grandparents left Baden-Baden a century earlier. I had looked at the Fulbright list from A through Z and decided on basic requirements: the water had to be drinkable; knowledge of the language would not be required; penicillin would cure most of what I might catch; and, since I wasn't sure of my ability to function abroad, it had to be for one semester. Two places met the requirements: provincial Portugal and metropolitan Budapest. I was homesick for a city, and duty in Communist Europe paid better.

In the days since I had landed and was deposited, confused and groggy, at the flat I shared with a pleasant young couple with one child and no English, I managed not to starve to death only because I found a cafeteria a few doors away. After I found my way to the American embassy, bought a detailed map and guidebook, and learned how to get a monthly transport pass, I felt a little better about being able to manage the external details of my life.

On the afternoon of my birthday, however, that didn't seem comforting enough. But then I looked down at the sweep of the not-at-all-blue Danube, from Margaret Island past the ornate Parliament and the mustard-yellow buildings of central Pest and the Chain Bridge directly below me and downriver past Gellert Hill and three more bridges toward Csepel Island. Did I mind being a year older? Not particularly. Had I enjoyed people dutifully celebrating my recent birthdays? Not at all. Was someone who felt sorry for himself while looking at that view and every opportunity it promised worse than pathetic? Obviously.

In the days and months that followed, though, I checked in almost daily at the embassy for mail and a look at the most recent week-old *International Herald Tribune*, I moved farther and farther outward, translating key words from *Fokusz*, the weekly calendar of events, using a larger and more detailed map to trace my route on a bus or trolley to the end of one line and onto another: to the top of the highest Buda hill to the west; to the grounds of the international trade fair, with goods from Albania and other countries then barred from American markets, on the outskirts of Pest to the east; to the Margaret Kovacs Museum, full of grotesque clay figures, in Szentendre to the north; and, on a one-track trolley line, where motor-men exchanged the switch key, to Nagyteteny to the south, where few of my Hungarian friends and no one from the embassy had ever been.

In the process, I discovered that my reading knowledge of French was a lot better than I thought, if Hungarian was the alternative, and that, if addressed in German, at that time the local alternative of choice, I could pidgin my way through simple transactions. In Hungarian, I learned to say please, thank you very much, sorry, and vay-tsay, which means water closet. I learned to count to ten and even higher, though in speaking I never needed a number higher than three. My only verb was the one in the sentence that translates into "I don't speak Hungarian." But every normal human contact was difficult, like walking through knee-deep water.

The most useful word I learned, with heavy emphasis on the first syllable, was "Amerikai." This was the best response to gestures, raised eyebrows, and unintelligible questions in Hungarian and German. Most of the time, this answer seemed to account for my odd behavior or bemusement, for in 1981 the average Hungarian did not encounter many Americans. The response of people who didn't speak English was usually—I am guessing here—something like "Ah, how interesting." Those who did speak English wanted to share their knowledge of the States, find out why my English was so different from what they had heard on the BBC, Radio Free Europe, and instructional tapes, or learn more about the alien and exotic capitalist world.

Small talk, mostly geographical and climatological, was easiest to deal with. Questions about my mid-south-western American accent raised unpleasant memories of condescending easterners in my own country, but usually I was able to deflect them by a discussion of dialectal variation in a very, very large country.

Once a student asked how it felt to live in a socialist society. From my very limited point of view, I said, it didn't seem to matter. In a city of two million people, somebody had to be responsible for clean water, transportation, garbage disposal, and all the other services we take for granted. Whether that person was called a councilman or a commissar was not my immediate concern because I was having to worry about practical details I had never before had to think about.

Of course, the distinction mattered to my Hungarian colleagues and students at the university, most of whom were careful not to go too often to the library at the English embassy and would not even use the one at the American embassy. I met Gyorgy Konrad, a writer then so deep in official disapproval that he dared to come to the house of the American press and culture advisor because even that couldn't make things any worse. He said that the authorities would not, as before, necessarily arrest you for speaking out—but they let you know that they could if they wanted to. Once, after a lecture in the provinces, I was asked if I thought I were being followed by the secret police. "I don't know," I said. "I never looked." My colleagues in Budapest never asked this question, though it was not clear whether they were less or more paranoid than the man in Szeged. At any rate, I had no intention of trying to overthrow the evil Communist empire single-handedly, partly because it was too hard, partly because I was conscious of being a guest and not wanting to "make problems" (a staple of Hungarian English) for my friends, but mostly because I realized that I was representing my country not only in my teaching but every time I left my flat—and possibly, though I had few visitors, inside it as well.

Even as I expanded my knowledge of Budapest and of Hungarian culture and history, I began to circle inward and backward—not physically but psychically. For one thing, I was teaching nothing but American literature, which I had done part of the time for years, and, in a course which had no syllabus, no requirements, and very little attendance, American Civilization and Culture, subjects that I had never thought much about.

I discovered that I was eager to think about them, or at least remember and feel about them in unaccustomed ways, and I reacted to my country and my past like someone a long way from home who hears not just a familiar language but a familiar accent, no matter what the content. In consequence, I began to read, proportionately, more American prose than at any other period in my life.

And even some poetry. A few years earlier, one of my best friends had been a poet, but I put up with the poetry because he was a good man. Otherwise, I read poetry only in anthologies I used when I couldn't escape teaching a survey course. But when an American poet, Robert Hass, came to Budapest on a P.E.N. tour, I offered my services as tour guide, read eagerly and with pleasure the volume of poems he gave me, and invited him to visit my classes.

In one of them he asked the group to write a poem on the spur of the moment. I hadn't been on the student side of the podium in twenty years, and I had been looking out the window. Prodded into activity, I scribbled the first thing that came into my head:

> *The Danube flows past ancient ruins.*
> *Ten minutes to go.*

When I read it aloud, Hass was a little taken aback, but he recovered, and he deserves credit, if that is what attached to it, for initiating my subsequent career as a poet.

Some directions I took were less exotic. True, what was familiar to me was exotic to my students and colleagues. For example, I conducted the Hungarian premiere of *Shane*—the audience particularly liked the dog—and, invited to contribute to an issue of *Acta Litteraria Academicae Scientiarum Hungaricae,* a terminally Eurocentric title, I chose to write about *The Virginian.* It was my second article on the American Western, in which I had maintained a sheepish and secret interest after I was supposed to have outgrown childish things, and it made me realize that there was more to say on the subject. Ten years later the pair of essays had grown into a book. Asked to give a lecture to the English Club on short notice, I said that of course I could talk about jazz. Or, if they wanted, American country and western music, which I had spent my first twenty years trying to escape and the rest regarding as a source of low-camp, condescending humor. The response was so enthusiastic that I realized that there might be something intellectually interesting in the topic. But mostly, surrounded by the high culture of middle Europe, I responded to the homely quality of the songs about discreditable behavior and very human emotions. Alone in my flat, I played "Red River Valley" on the Red Chinese harmonica I had bought in a music store in Pest, partly because it is one of the few things I can play (the opening of the last movement of Beethoven's Ninth is another), partly because I had lived not far from the sandy bottom and thin trickle of the Red River for more than a decade.

I didn't know the Red River well enough to miss it. I had grown up on a very different kind of river, the Missouri, and I hadn't thought about that in years either. But now I was confronted daily by a far more famous and altogether classier river, the Danube. My American correspondents were impressed. I mentioned in a letter to a friend the simple fact that the water level of the river was low, and he wrote back enthusiastically, "The Danube is low? What a statement. You're in Hungary! On the Danube! Can you believe it? I cannot."

Robert Hass said much the same thing while we were walking across the Sabadsag Bridge in the soft October twilight toward the Gellert Hotel: "Two country boys walking across the Danube. It is hard to believe." In fact, he is from San Francisco, regarded by Americans and Europeans as one of the most cosmopolitan and exotic places in the United States, but in imagination he felt as rustic as I, the former boy from Boonville, Missouri.

It took a while to adjust to the fact of the Danube, as opposed to the myth. I could see it every time I looked out my seventh-floor window. But I had reservations about the Danube: it sounded too pretty to be serious, though in fact it is as brown and polluted as any midwestern American river. When I first saw it in Budapest, I was conscious that it was not so much a river as a space, providing incomparable perspective for viewing the buildings on both banks, like a gigantic reflecting pool designed by a landscape architect of genius. In fact, the new visitor to Budapest is continually distracted from the river to the setting: at night, by the lights along the ramparts and across the Chain Bridge; during the day, by the Castle and other monuments, which compel the eye upward, or by the end of Margaret Island, which leads the gaze down toward the city center. But at first, living in downtown Pest, I had little sense of the river *as* river. Nothing in my experience prepared me for a body of water that one could approach by what must surely be the world's widest flight of steps. Nothing between Sabadsag Bridge and Margaret Island gave the impression that the Danube was anything but a very large stretch of ornamental water.

The boats seemed ornamental too. Excursion boats are too pretty for my subconscious taste, and I never really believed in the hydrofoils; even if they work on the Danube, they would not make three bends in the Missouri without heading across a corn field and into somebody's barn.

Nevertheless, I felt the influence of the river. On my first walk across the Chain Bridge, I too thought, "I'm really walking across the Danube." But it took a while for me to accept the Danube as a real river and as a part of my life. Rising in the early dawn, it was the first thing I saw, the lights of Margaret Island gleaming off the west channel. I began to plan my trips to the university to include a walk across a bridge, usually the Elizabeth Bridge, because even if the Danube wasn't real, it was lovely, and being suspended in space gave me a sense of openness and freedom that in my less arthritic but more acrophobic younger days I never experienced on the bridge at Boonville.

Yet paradoxically, living on the Danube returned a part of my life I had forgotten. Crossing the Elizabeth Bridge one day, I glanced at the river and thought, "It is rising. There must have been a lot of rain upstream." Only then did I realize that I knew this because a large tree limb—the first flotsam I had seen in the Danube—was moving rapidly downstream. Later, on my first trip to Visegrad, I stood at the wall of the citadel looking out over the river—certainly a real river for me by now—and heard a companion ask about the configuration of sandbars; without thinking, I gave the answer from my long-buried knowledge of the Missouri. Obuda and Csepel Islands were industrialized enough even for one accustomed to the last sweep of the Missouri at Kansas City before it absorbs the Kansas River with its steel mills and refineries. Szent Endre Island seemed long and lazy enough for a hundred Jackson's Islands, Mark Twain's or the one, now absorbed into the shore, opposite Boonville, to which I gave that name in my imagination. And at Nagyteteny the Danube seems as deserted as some of the minor tributaries of the Missouri I remember from my youth. Best of all, an old map at the Castle Museum revealed that Margaret Island was once two islands, and this change convinced me that the Danube was a real, serious river in terms my life in small-town Missouri had given me.

More important, though it took a little longer, I began to see that these terms could be valid in more than a geographical sense, that it was important for me to remember and understand them. And, after a decade of fumbling with forgotten language and subject matter, to begin the process of recovering a world, of learning to listen to the almost forgotten rhythms of my regional idiom, and of realizing and recreating a self which I had tried for years to escape.

Once a Hungarian asked a pointed question about my views of a controversial American foreign policy. Without thinking, I had answered that I felt about my country the way I felt about my father: I didn't always agree with him, and sometimes I was ashamed of him. But that is where I came from. That didn't go in my report to the Fulbright office, though it was the most important thing I learned in Budapest.

YOU COULDA BEEN A
CONTENDER

Early in 1991 I had just revised *Mid-Lands,* a reminiscent social history about growing up in a postwar midwestern small town. Carrying the manuscript, boxed to send it back to the publisher, I stopped by my chairman's office. He was new to the department, curious about what its members were doing, and very enthusiastic about any signs of intellectual or academic life.

He asked what I was carrying, and I not only told him but showed him. Without taking the manuscript from the box, he picked up a swatch of pages here, a swatch there, and scanned what he found. Then he let the manuscript fall back, looked up, and said, "This will change your whole life."

I was ready for a change. Not that I was unhappy with my career: I have a modest reputation—international, as far as it goes—for my scholarly work on Evelyn Waugh. Articles on this and other subjects have been published and reviewed in four countries outside the United States, even in magazines that appear on selected newsstands and have prices on the covers. It is not written in high Mandarin style, but it had moved so far from my native dialect that one correspondent thought I was an Englishman. On the other hand, a colleague advocating plain English for scholarly work once remarked, "Now take Davis. He writes stuff that a wife can understand."

This colleague also said, in response to *Mid-Lands,* that now I was a *real* writer. My current chairman used the same words. In a later conversation, he added, "I'm surprised you didn't become a journalist."

"I did," I replied. Like everything I say, this was the truth, though it needs a little modification and involves, in the oral style I learned from my grandfather, a good deal of backing and filling. In high school, I thought that the only way to become a writer was to serve an apprenticeship as a newspaperman—the Hemingway syndrome. Therefore, I had quit my job at the local Dairy Queen to take another, with a pay cut of over fifty percent, on the *Cooper County Record.* I had planned to be a journalism major at the University of Missouri, but I got a last-minute scholarship offer from Rockhurst College, at that time a liberal arts school. Since Rockhurst had no journalism program, I did the next best thing and became an English major.

However, Rockhurst did have a college newspaper, and I became a reporter, columnist, editor, and for one year a scab printer. After graduation, I took a job with the *Great Bend Daily Tribune* to cover sports and general news and to take an occasional photo. That lasted three months, until I got an offer of a graduate assistantship at the University of Kansas.

So I was telling my chairman the truth. Why, he wanted to know, had I given it up? This attitude, from someone in the same racket, I found rather puzzling.

However, it was easy to answer his question. "Because it was boring." Not at first, and not always even then. But sooner rather than later, and more often than not. After I began graduate school—when the only time you heard the word "Mentor" was in a discussion of the *Odyssey*—I was suffering from a sense of inferiority, which none of my colleagues tried to dispel. At this point, I read Grantland Rice's autobiography. Most people have probably never heard of Grantland Rice, which shows that there is some progress. He was the founder of modern sportswriting and its most famous practitioner well into the 1950s. He wrote his book from the pinnacle of success in a mood of complete self-satisfaction. And as I read the book, I could think only, "What an awful way to spend your life."

So I turned down the offer to apply for the job of sports editor of a morning newspaper in Joplin, Missouri, and slogged ahead as a graduate student, doing the kind of reading and writing one did in the late fifties and early sixties, and then up through the academic ranks and a variety of publications, none of them remotely like what I had written as an undergraduate or beginning journalist.

Not, that is, until someone offered me an incentive to do so. In the fall of 1981, I was a Fulbright lecturer in Budapest—the only Fulbrighter in the country, in fact, in the days before Hungary was overrun by Peace Corps volunteers, squads of Fulbrighters, Billy Graham, *Playboy*, and hordes of junketing congresspersons. We were still trying to persuade the Hungarians—those allowed to and brave enough to talk to Americans—that the American Way of Life was desirable and wholesome.

To assist in this noble work, the State Department put out, in the Warsaw Pact countries that would allow it, a magazine called *U.S.A.* Most of the articles were reprints, but a section was written specially for each country. Prospective authors were warned to be innocuous: descriptions of nature and comparisons of American and local customs were allowed; keep it light; be positive.

Hardly the kind of thing that twenty-five years in academia had prepared me to write. But this was my first trip to Europe, and I was still bemused by the glamour of Abroad and rather proud of my ability to function there. So I tried to think of a subject—in vain, until I realized that I ran, or walked or rode, across one every day—the Danube. And I had grown up on the Missouri, much less famous, but at least as wide. What I knew about rivers—their rise and fall, their idiosyncrasies, the traffic along them—I had unconsciously applied every day.

The article about my impressions of the two rivers was far easier to write than even the shortest review of a scholarly book. And the pay was proportionately better than for anything else I had published—even if I couldn't read it when it appeared in Hungarian. Moreover, the response to the article was quicker and more positive than for any scholarly endeavor. My Hungarian friends praised it warmly and—they are a critical bunch—I think sincerely. The editors reported that the translator enjoyed his work more than usual. An ex-wife said it was the best thing I'd ever done. One of my children even read it.

What the hell, I thought: if it's that easy, I'll do some more. But it wasn't that easy a second time: *U.S.A.* didn't like the other pieces I tried. A later attempt to sell travel articles proved harder than I expected—I put in too much atmosphere in proportion to fact, I suppose—and I soon gave up hope for that as a second career and major tax break.

A year or so later, trying to sort out my reactions to Paris, I tried another piece, this time about leaving my home town for the big city in wider and wider swings. In first and subsequent drafts, I had gone back to the tone I had used in my undergraduate journalism— "smartass" is a good way to describe it, full of easy irony and a kind of irritating knowingness. A Hungarian friend to whom I showed a draft didn't like it at all.

So I put it away and did some other things, including writing some poems. One benefit of writing poetry, even if it isn't very good, is that you haven't got much time to fiddle around with fancy effects, and if you do, you have to learn to take them out. And you have to decide who you are and how you are going to sound.

Finally, after some more false starts, I produced a draft of the piece about going to the city, which seemed more or less satisfactory. Then I didn't know what to do with it—I only knew about academic markets—until I saw a notice about a special issue of *North Dakota Quarterly* on "Travel and Travail." Robert W. Lewis published it. Then, of course, came the question that every writer dreads: "What next?"

In my case, next was a series of academic and scholarly pieces, some of them commissioned. But I had broken into my past, and the next personal essay, about playing small-town baseball, came easier. Then, after a third trip to Europe, in a rush of five weeks, I wrote another sixty percent of *Mid-Lands*. The last twenty percent came in revision—the stage in which I discovered what the book was about and what principle of internal form shaped it. Both surprised me.

I made some other discoveries that may not surprise anyone else but that are important to me not only as a writer but as a teacher. Even before I thought of writing *Mid-Lands* or any part of it, I had begun to feel dissatisfied with the kind of writing I had been doing. Partly this resulted from the fact that, in 1981, I had finished the book toward which my career had been pointing for twenty years. And when I looked up from that project, I saw references to "post-structuralism." "Post?" Hell, I hadn't even heard about structuralism. I had missed a whole movement. How could I ever catch up?

An older colleague, now dead, once said that the advantage of getting older is that you realize that you don't have to go. On the other hand, I wasn't ready to stop entirely because I still enjoyed reading and got a real rush from writing about what I read. And it occurred to me that the critics whose work I read and even re-read for pleasure—George Orwell, Edmund Wilson, Dwight MacDonald are some examples—did not write academic prose.

I had, very gingerly, already begun to write essays outside my field—modern British fiction. Most of these were about contemporary novels that played variations on pulp fiction's version of the Western myth. While I thought of writing more and making them into a book, I treated the idea more like a retirement fantasy than a serious project. At least I did until I had to use it as a pretext for a sabbatical leave.

Faced with actually writing the book on the Western, I realized that I was less interested in what the novelists said or meant than in what they meant to someone who had grown up watching B movies and had heard his father talk about Tom Mix and embody some of the virtues of the fictional westerner and not a few of the faults of a real one. Writing the book—at least the beginning and end and some of the transitions—forced me to think about who I was and why I was that way.

When I finished a draft of that book, *Playing Cowboys,* I took off for a semester in eastern Hungary, where mostly I thought about America and even got around to reading *Walden.* But I thought more about a time and place and some people in my life than I did about books. I had spent a lot of time trying to get away from Boonville, Missouri, and my education and experience had encouraged and even demanded that I do so. I knew where Boonville stood with the outside world, and, as the years passed, I stopped mentioning where I was from and what my family did and thought, forgetting that I had learned a great deal, a lot earlier, from them.

But, as I discovered as my family's numbers dwindled and expanded, I never got away from it. It doesn't have any scholars but me, but it has a strong sense of style, with storytellers on both sides. Their values, I was surprised to discover, had shaped my career, academic and otherwise. I am the oldest member of the extended family and its chief storyteller and wanderer. It's easier than opening the latest intellectual CARE package from Paris. And it's a lot more fun. Besides, *Mid-Lands* didn't have to have a bibliography or an index.

The real issue—the one implied by my chairman—is whether I had been wasting my time for the previous thirty-five years, fourteen scholarly books, and hundred or so articles. There are two ways to answer that.

One, of which my father would approve, is practical. Without a tenured professorship, I wouldn't have had the leisure to look back at my experience—or been able to go to Hungary. And I certainly wouldn't have had the sabbatical time to devote to writing *Mid-Lands* and part of a summer to begin to plan the sequel and another in the New Mexico mountains to write a draft.

A second way of answering the question is intellectual. If I had gone to Hungary after twenty-five years as a journalist—no matter how successful—I would have seen Hungary. But I might not have seen anything else, especially not myself seeing Hungary. And from that perspective I was able, after many false starts, to find something to say about myself and not about some writer. Some *other* writer.

But all those writers—Waugh, Hemingway, Graham Greene, and on and on—helped me to find the perspective on my own experience and to discover my own voice. They are as much a part of my experience as a five-week stay in Paris. In fact, I've spent a lot more time with Waugh, so much that my daughter thought for a long time that he was an adult version of an imaginary friend. And apparently I still believe—even after writing a book about them—in some of the platitudes given me years ago about the value of a liberal education.

That's an old-fashioned term, but then I'm getting to be old-fashioned myself. I know that I'm not going to learn the new terms and ideologies that supplanted those I learned in graduate school and since. I hope it's not because I'm lazy, or lazier than anybody else, but because I have something more interesting to say, at least to me.

My chairman was wrong: *Mid-Lands* didn't change my life in any obvious ways. It didn't make me rich or famous, and I taught in Oklahoma until I retired.

Of course, the fact that I wrote the book changed the way I looked at myself and my teaching as well as my writing. It helped me to discover the obvious fact that lives have meaning even if they haven't been processed through someone else's book or theory. And though the unexamined life may not be worth living, or in fact lived, all of us do a good deal of examining, like it or not.

A surprising number of academics feel the same way. I had scarcely gotten registered at my first Western Literature Association meeting before I met three other people with strong scholarly credentials who had turned to personal writing. The following year, I chaired a session on the topic and drew a large and responsive crowd.

Personal writing isn't the only kind that scholars can turn to. Recently, though they start from very different points, Ted Solotaroff ("The Literary Campus and the Person of Letters," in *A Few Good Voices in My Head*) and Harold Fromm (*Academic Capitalism & Literary Value*) have called for a revival of the "person of letters," literate intellectuals who comment in readable style on a wide range of topics. Solotaroff, who is not primarily an academic, has a touching and thoroughly impractical scheme for a graduate program on the topic. Fromm, who got his Ph.D. from Wisconsin when it *was* Wisconsin, thinks that intelligent and flexible writers with academic training can and should do the job. But to be flexible, he implies, you have to have not just a theory to apply but a center from which to move.

The process of writing *Mid-Lands* and *Playing Cowboys*—and it was essentially the same process—has assured me that what I say, and how I say it, is . . . well, *fun*. That seems to me worth communicating. I'm not ready to give up writing about books, even for an academic audience. But I don't need the validation of an explicit theory or critical position, and the audience I seek doesn't either. I suspect that there are more of us than there are hard-line theorists. Perhaps I am so old-fashioned that, like wide ties, I have become avant-garde.

FATHERS AND SONS

I don't quite remember what led up to the question, but I think my son, nearing his mid-thirties, was trying to get some kind of understanding of our relationship. As is his habit (and mine) he doesn't approach that sort of thing directly, so he asked, "What kind of father was Grandpa? We only knew him as a grandfather."

Easier to ask than to answer. I could have told him to re-read my *Mid-Lands: A Family Album*, about my growing up in Boonville, Missouri, which, I realized while reading page proofs, was really about my father. But I couldn't think of much else.

But the question stuck in my mind, and a few months later, at a family reunion, I mentioned it to my daughter. She laughed and told a story about a visit with her cousins to the grave of my mother, whom none of them remembered. My sister and brother and I are separated, in ascending order, by gaps of five years. My daughter had said that according to what she'd heard from me, her grandmother had been really cool. My brother's daughters said that she sort of just seemed there. The daughter of my sister, who had fled to the convent rather than stay at home, said that she sounded like a real bitch. (My sister, on hearing this, said that she had told her daughter that Mom was just like her.)

My daughter's story reminded me that temporal perspective is crucial in these matters, and that my brother and sister would have different views. I know that as an adult my brother had difficulties with Dad because he stayed in Boonville and did things that Dad knew about and could criticize. I also know that my sister could always handle Dad in ways that his sons couldn't. But they have their own stories, and to try to answer my son's question, I began to arrange memories and stories, which for the Davises are pretty much indistinguishable.

For as long as I can remember, I knew about my father's early view of me. When I was born, in Lyons, Kansas, in the middle of the Dust Bowl, he was selling insurance door to door, and my mother said that sometimes he would drop by the house on his rounds, look at me in the crib, and leave without her knowing he had been there.

I could believe that because, when he reached grandfather age, he said, "I sure do like them little old babies." But as far as my actual memories went, he didn't seem all that interested in older children.

To be fair, he did try to do fatherly things with me, and I suspect that he was frustrated by failure. I was short, skinny, bookish, near-sighted, and clearly not the son of a man so tough that he never had to prove it and who, as young man, had thrown his older brother down the stairs for sassing their mother. I, on the other hand, lost a lot of playground fights, and not gracefully or stoically. Once he tried to show me how to throw an effective punch—"Act like you're hitting *through* the chin"—but I continued to lose fights until, after a sudden growth spurt that paralleled his own a quarter-century earlier, I got big enough that no one wanted to fight me.

Still, he tried to do conventional fatherly things, taking me hunting and fishing and into the country to look at cows and farms he might want to buy. But I was clearly not interested in cows and not much interested in the country. The few times we went hunting, I was mostly too young to use a gun safely, too short to keep pace with him in the field, and too cold to enjoy the experience even if I'd had the arms and the legs. The only hunting expedition I enjoyed was shooting from the car at rabbits in the fence-rows, and then I had to listen to him complain about dressing out the only rabbit (or anything else) I ever shot. It was running away from me, and by luck I hit it just under the tail with a .22 bullet.

The weather was warmer for fishing trips, but I didn't have the necessary patience or attention span, and the only thing that saved an all-night expedition—hot, sleepless, insect-filled, and nothing interesting to eat or (at that age) to drink—was my discovering on a trot-line a six-pound blue catfish. Dad was much happier dressing that, and the meat tasted as good as anything I've ever eaten.

One thing we both enjoyed was going to Kansas City to the fruit and vegetable market, where he bought supplies for the wholesale business from which he supplied grocers in a radius of thirty miles or so. We'd rise at two and get there about sunrise. Then he'd give me breakfast money and turn me loose to feel very adventurous and adult on my own.

In my early teens, he seemed to pay little attention to me unless he was giving orders—often preceded with "While you're resting, go out and" clean the barn or cut fence-row or mow grass or do something that I wouldn't have done on my own, or at all without pressure from someone I knew enough not to argue with.

He may have gone to my recitals and school plays, though I only remember Mom mentioning them. He wasn't the PTA type, but few men were in the 1940s. Neither he nor Mom came to my baseball and basketball games, but I didn't mind that because vocal parents were embarrassing to their offspring and a cause of derision to their teammates. Besides, not many parents of that era were that involved in their children's extra-curricular activities.

But he did teach me to play cards, mostly rummy, with the invaluable side effect of showing me that some people were a lot more skilled than I was, though I later discovered that not many people were as skilled as he was. Also, he had some interest in sports, as long as I wasn't playing. When I was a Tenderfoot Scout, someone discovered that Scout troops, accompanied by an adult, were allowed to usher at University of Missouri football games. He volunteered to take me and my friends to the games, and did so in a Ford woody of uncertain 1930s vintage (this was 1946, and cars were hard to come by) with roll-down shades on the sides. He'd let us off and disappear until the game ended. Again, he had sense enough to leave us alone.

Later he bought season tickets to the University of Missouri basketball games, and those too were good times, as man-to-man as we ever got.

Dad did notice when I became valedictorian of my high school graduating class—mostly, Mom suspected, because that was one in the eye of his slightly older brother, who all their lives had claimed intellectual superiority. And word from Arkansas City cast doubts on his paternity.

The one area in which he took a sometimes inconvenient interest was my religious training and practice. I remember him holding a copy of the blue-backed Baltimore Catechism and listening to my attempts to reproduce what the nuns thought were the right answers. He would also roust me out of bed every weekday morning to go to daily Mass. But he went to church only when one of his children was being baptized, confirmed, or married. He had no religious or as far as I could tell spiritual tendencies. His one concession to religion was the habit of carrying a medal with the supposed image of St. Christopher even after the Church decommissioned that entirely legendary figure. Given his driving habits—more attentive to cattle and crops than to the road even when he was sober—he must have figured he needed the protection.

His concern for my religious upbringing was legalistic rather than spiritual. When he married Mom in the rectory of Redemptorist parish in Kansas City in what may still be called a mixed marriage, he had promised to raise any children as Catholics. And to him a contract was a contract, whatever his other failings.

And he had some. He was what he called a periodic drunk. For months at a time, he wouldn't touch a drop. Then, for no reason even Mom could figure, he would disappear until he finished drinking or it finished him. Sometimes, before I was in my teens, I was taken as cover for, or sent by my mother to prevent, impromptu drinking bouts. I would be left in the car, bookless, alone, and even on familiar ground afraid to leave because I never knew when he could come back. I discovered that it is possible to be bored and frightened at the same time.

These episodes were less worrisome but to me more inconvenient than his full-scale drunks, when he would disappear for what seemed like days at a time, impatient of family constraints or ashamed to have us see him. In my later teens, I was sent to the basement to get him to come to bed at the end of a bout and found him sitting in an old chair in the dark, looking, as I thought then, like a ruined king. He motioned for me to leave. I wasn't anxious to stay.

Once he tried to have harmless adult fun in the house. Mom had gone somewhere, and he brought two strange men home with him. One began to play pretty fair ragtime on the old piano in the dining room. You can't play ragtime *pianissimo*, of course, and later I came to like that kind of music. But I had to get up at 6 A.M. next day to milk a cow, and, as I discovered when I had my own, adolescents have an unpredictable tendency to be censorious about the pleasures of their parents. So I complained, and the piano shut down for the night. Not long after, I felt guilty about interfering with pleasure as innocent as I can remember Dad having. Still do.

Today, in the expansion that the term has undergone as result of feminism, sensitivity movements, and therapy, his behavior would be called abusive. We didn't think of it that way in the 1940s. He was never violent when drinking, at least at home or as far as we knew outside it, and when he punished us, he did so with great deliberation and mostly with justice.

He was pretty strict about relatively minor matters, and once Mom said that he was being too hard on me. "Look, Babe," he replied, "I been there and I know." (This was the corollary, I realized, to a more frequent injunction: "Don't do as I do. Do as I say.") Nobody doubted that he did know. He didn't look or act like the fathers of my friends, farmers or small businessmen. He'd been an oil field roughneck after he'd worked in a bootlegger's cover business, and he'd done a lot of other things. My brother suspects some lurid episodes in his past, but anyone who might have known about them, if they existed, is dead. Anyway, he was obviously not someone to mess with—wiry and lean until his fifties, unsmiling, with fewer words than Gary Cooper.

One of the few times I saw him in a public role was at my brother's wedding dance at the Rod and Gun Club near Boonville. A deputy sheriff reported that an escaped convict might be in the area and could represent a danger. The two fathers, both tanned from the outdoors but otherwise different in every conceivable way, went on alert, took charge, and became the focus of the whole group—without moving or saying a word. In the dining car on the train back to Chicago, my urban, Yankee wife and I sat across from a soft, pleasant, salesman whom you couldn't even call pale. My wife, who existed in total and mutual incomprehension with Dad, remarked on the contrast between this man and the two at the dance: unlike him, they could be dangerous.

But he didn't try to act dangerous. He just was. He was even more uncomfortable with expressions of emotion. When my mother's father was killed in a car-train accident in Florida, he went with her brother to make funeral arrangements and to take care of Grandma. That was practical and necessary. But when, the night before the funeral, Mom and I sat in the living room drinking whiskey and mourning, he came in and brusquely ordered us to bed rather than sit there drinking and carrying on. The most he would say, years later, when Grandpa was mentioned, was, "I sure do miss that old man." And after Mom died, he took care of her mother, though the last time I went with him to visit her in a nursing home, after she had sunk into dementia, we got as far as a restaurant. As we left, he said, "I just can't do it." That was the only time I ever heard him admit defeat.

As a young man, I certainly didn't object to people thinking my father was tough, though I never got into the kind of "My dad can lick your dad" playground challenge. Maybe I didn't have to. And he didn't have to demonstrate that he was tough; he just was. This reputation persisted into his old age. My daughter and her cousin, probably early teenagers, went to the Dairy Queen and were approached by two young men. It wasn't clear what they were after, but they asked about the girls' family, and when they heard the name of M. C. Davis, they left. My daughter, telling the story more than twenty years later after the fact and a dozen years after Dad's death, was still impressed that he carried that kind of weight.

Perhaps she was remembering the time, when, sitting in our living room, I told her and her siblings stories of my father's youthful career. Some of it can be traced—prize fighting for travel money to get to New Mexico; being abandoned by his older sister in the New Mexico desert and by a Hispanic boy in the New Mexico mountains for being a smartass; leaving high school to roughneck in the oil fields of the Texas Panhandle; having his station in the Kansas City dry cleaner's blown up because of late protection money; getting stopped at a roadblock for Pretty Boy Floyd. There were hints of other stories: the scar on his cheek he wouldn't talk about at all but reportedly came from a fight with a Mexican girl's large and jealous boyfriend; the midnight crash of the Arkansas City streetcar, supposedly safe in the barn, into the canal at the foot of Summit Street. My fascinated daughter said, "You make Grandpa sound like he was a hood." From across the room her mother, one of nature's schoolmarm defenders of civilization, said, "Your grandfather is *still* a hood."

Dad's youthful indiscretions turned out to have unexpected advantages for me. As I said, he was very hard on minor lapses and indiscretions, but when I got into real trouble, he got me out of it with a lack of fuss at which I was astonished and for which I was grateful. (My son may have wondered why I was similarly tolerant of some of his errors. It's hard to condemn too seriously stupidities that one has committed decades earlier.)

When I left home for college, he seemed to take little interest in my career there, though he did come to a father-son banquet and to my graduation. My graduate school career seemed to puzzle him. "Are you ever going to stop going to school?" he would ask, sometimes in words, sometimes by attitude. When I got my first full-time academic job, he and Mom came to visit my wife and me in Chicago. I had to tell him not to make eye contact on the subway, and he was as excited as a child at seeing the sea-going freighters tied up at Navy Pier on Chicago's lakefront. The only other thing I remember from that visit was his buying me a paint-scraper to get the sloppily applied paint off the glass in the windows. Later Mom reported his saying, of my wife, "That poor little girl." He may have been worried about our financial stability. I don't know how well he understood women. He certainly underestimated his daughter-in-law, who was as small and probably as tough as his own mother who, judging from his older sister's stories and a few surviving letters, was a ringtailed bitch.

Later in my professional life he seemed to take the view that while he had no idea what I was doing, I seemed to be getting away with it, and when I sandbagged with put-on country accent some wiseass urbanites who came into his store on the edge of town, he was clearly appreciative.

But we didn't know much about each other's lives. In fact, I maintained a careful incuriosity about what his life was like, especially his life with my mother. They did not seem affectionate, and as I went through my twenties, Mom was clearly less and less happy in the marriage. At one point, she almost explicitly asked my permission to divorce Dad and move to Kansas City. That was something I couldn't deal with, and said so.

Yet, when Mom's stomach cancer was discovered, too late for any kind of treatment, Dad stood up to the challenge. He was running a lucrative business near the interstate highway, but he sold it in order to allow Mom to stay at home as long as possible. He learned to care for her and give her shots for pain, and when she had to go to the hospital and I came back from California to take part, with my sister, in the vigil in her room (everyone else had to work), he took the overnight shift.

Once the hospital chaplain, a very unsympathetic-looking priest, came to Mom's room, stood at the end of the bed, and in a harsh voice delivered a brief sermon about Jesus loving and taking care of her as her husband had. When I started to protest, he waved me away and continued. As it turned out, he may have been right for all the wrong reasons.

One morning I was up at dawn, hours before I expected him. He came into the kitchen, wearier and more slumped than I'd ever seen him, and said, "Your mother died." He didn't give particulars, and I didn't ask for them. I can't remember if I hugged him in sympathy. I like to think that I did.

A year later, I moved to Oklahoma, a fairly easy day's drive from Boonville, and I saw more of him than I had in years. He stayed active, still trading a few cars and cattle but mostly running a very general store at the edge of town and managing the commercial property on the strip of land he'd developed. Part of it he sold, in an act of which he may have appreciated the irony, to Valley Hope, a facility for drying out alcoholics.

He didn't dry out, at least not for long. For example, he was sober when I came through, as I had arranged to do, on my way to a Masters swimming meet in St. Louis, but when I came back unexpectedly, he had disappeared on a drunk. (My God—I just realized that he was a few months older than I am now.) But as his stamina waned, the bouts got shorter.

Grandchildren had begun to appear by this time—ultimately, nine of them. My sister's children were wary of him—he lived just across the big back yard—but my children saw him perhaps once a year and as far as I could tell seemed to think him indulgent if inarticulate. I remember him sitting in his kitchen with my first child on his lap, feeding her bacon. She wasn't hungry, but she opened her mouth to each morsel until her cheeks bulged, both of them more interested in the process than in the result.

By this time, we had reached a kind of détente. I would call him, but our conversations dealt with information, not feelings. The one exception was when I told him that my wife had asked me to move out. He may not have grunted, but that was the impression I retain, and then he offered to come to Oklahoma to be with me. Knowing how he hated to travel, at least when sober, I was touched, but I declined. Perhaps I shouldn't have.

Before my divorce, my wife said that I was getting more and more like him—and she did not mean it as a compliment. Perhaps she saw that I worked a lot, though I was much more involved with my children than he was with his, that I could be brusque, that moderation was foreign to my nature, and most probably that my drinking was getting out of hand. Since I didn't drink the way he did, I couldn't for a while see that there was a problem. I was enough like him to be able to quit for a while, though in my case it's been over twenty years. However, my wife did say, once, that I would have made a good pioneer, and on another occasion she admitted that while I had faults, at least I wasn't sneaky, so Dad did have some positive influence that she might not have perceived.

I'm not sure how Dad felt about my professional life, though others told me that he was proud of me. Once he came to pick me up after a meeting of graduate deans and assistants held near the Kansas City airport. He asked me what it was, and I gave him the full title of the group. He said "Okay," drawing it out in a way that showed that he might have been puzzled, but not overly impressed.

I'd send him copies of my books, especially an anthology of essays on John Steinbeck that I'd dedicated to him and to my grandfather, both resourceful and practical men who might have served as models for Steinbeck characters. I don't remember what he said, if anything, but at least I found it on his shelf after he died.

By this time he was in his mid-sixties, and semiretired. He spent more and more time in the little house that his father-in-law had converted from a carriage house (my nephew is remodeling it now), seeing a few surviving friends, still going on a drunk now and then, and occasionally taking a trip with a friend, once to Mexico, once to Las Vegas. I asked him how he did. "Made expenses," he said.

He could always cook—he and Mom had run restaurants—and he was particularly good with mashed potatoes, the best I've eaten except for some that cost $8 in a posh restaurant to which my son took me at the north end of Soho. That was his only dish that didn't have grease in it, though of course it had plenty of butter. He did his own housework. Once I offered to do the dishes, and he declined. "Dad," I said, "you ought to get a dishwasher." He shuffled his feet and ducked his head and said, "Ah, I don't want to get married again." I don't think he was joking. And he certainly never got married again, despite the importunities of several widows. He couldn't figure out why anyone would want "an old drunk."

He began to read more than I could have expected. He liked books with facts in them, like James Michener's, and he read through the local library's collection of mystery stories. When those ran out, I'd send him some I'd found at garage sales. On a visit I tried to interest him in George V. Higgins's *The Friends of Eddie Coyle*, which was filed with novels rather than with mysteries. He read a page, closed the book, and said, "That's nothing but a lot of nasty talking." I said that I was sorry that he was discovering the words, and he didn't say anything. Of course, he'd heard and no doubt used them, but he wasn't used to seeing them in print.

More often I'd send him tapes of music I thought he'd like, and I'd call him and, less frequently, write to him. Occasionally, he'd tell stories, sitting under the walnut trees he sometimes threatened to sell as timber but never did, and I took a photo of him, elbows on knees, peering rather peevishly over his glasses and under his cap. When I sent him a copy, he complained that it made him look old. "I just press the button," I said.

In his late sixties, his health began to fail. He had surgery for colon cancer after the doctor had to keep calling after the diagnosis and after he went on a drinking bout. A few years later he submitted to triple-bypass surgery after my sister threatened to have him declared incompetent if he kept refusing to go to the hospital. Even after the operation he insisted that the symptoms were nothing but indigestion. Then he overturned a tractor on himself while mowing a pasture on my brother's farm. My brother thought he was dead until he opened his eyes and said, "Anybody got a drink of whiskey?" A gear lever ran through his bicep, but the wound healed rapidly.

Then he set fire to his pants leg while burning brush and later cut the arch of his foot with a chainsaw. "Right to the bone," he said. "Dad," I answered, "there's nothing *but* bone there." We began to think that he was too tough and mean to get seriously hurt.

But in his late seventies, he developed symptoms that sent him back to the hospital for repair of an aneurysm and exploration of possible kidney problems. One kidney was blocked, the other cancerous. But he went home, and I drove up to stay with him while he recuperated.

I found an empty house, and no one answered the phone at my brother's or sister's. This time he wasn't on a drunk: he'd had a hemorrhage and was in the local hospital waiting transportation to the bigger facility in Columbia. I followed the ambulance, with him and my brother in it, and for at least a week the family took turns sitting in his screened-off cubicle in the Intensive Care Unit.

He had a good idea of how bad things were, and once he motioned me close and said, "Give me something." I knew what he meant, though I acted as though I didn't. In the first place, I didn't have what he wanted and probably needed, and in the second place, I wasn't tough enough to give it to him if I'd had it.

In the long hours beside his bed, I'd read for a while, check my pulse against the monitor, partly out of boredom, partly to see if I was still healthy (60 or lower resting rate), and look at Dad's profile. My daughter, now too old and dignified to store bacon in her cheeks, came to see him and later reproached me for not telling Dad that I loved him.

But later I put my impressions into a poem, "Lines of Descent."

> *The lines in front draw different:*
> *your forehead etched by circumstance and sun*
>   *three lines across,*
>   *mine arrowed inward pushed by other strains;*
> *your nose sloped downward to a broader swell,*
>   *mine upward at the point*

carved out by other genes;
my teeth, thank God and Grandma Murray, grew
from other roots than yours.

Looked at the other way, I am your son:
legs built short to lever from the ground,
weight of shoulder, torso's length,
long spine stiff against the strain
the world and we put on it.

I sent a copy to my sister, who showed it to Dad, who said, "He certainly has a way with words."

He didn't, but he made it quite clear that he wanted no further medical treatment. I continued to call him until the conversations got too depressing for both of us, and then I wrote chatty, factual letters that did more to ease my sense of obligation than his mood, which grew darker and darker. A few months later he hemorrhaged again, was taken to the hospital, and died two and a half months short of his eightieth birthday, his survival that long a triumph of heredity over environment.

When I called people to announce his death, a woman friend wondered if he'd left enough to cover the funeral. As long as it didn't cost more than $300,000, I said. "What? I thought he lived on his Social Security." "Probably he did," I said, "but that's just the way he was." My ex-wife sympathized because, in her view, I had all these unresolved issues with him. That was long ago, I said.

Four years later, alone in the New Mexico mountains he'd loved as a youth, I managed to sort my feelings in a poem he wouldn't be able to read, called "A Forest Requiem."

The day you died I acted as you lived:
Got up and did my job and made the calls
to cover absence, check arrival times,
get clearer schedules of your final moves
than, living, you would leave.

The children thought I did not mourn enough.
The ex-wife thought I could not deal with grief
at losing problems that I had not solved.

I could not solve or put a Kleenex to
what learning, blood, or love could not delay.

The plains we came from
gave us horizons as a goal and spur
to more horizons, movement as an end.

Here pines and aspens measure only time.
Fallen or felled, the trees decay in lines
tracing their growth and girth,
shadows of strength and substance.

The photo of him, which I referred to as the complaint department, hung on my office wall for years. I mentioned it to my brother, who said, "It'd take a pretty bold student to get that far." Now it hangs, looking at me over the computer screen, in my home office.

But that was only one image. A few years after he died, I went through some family letters that his older sister had kept, along with everything else that had come into her hands. Dad, long before he was a father, had written to her when he was about twelve, hoping to go to New Mexico for a visit, perhaps to live, but, he added in another letter, "Maybe i might not pass in school if i don't ma won't let me come. it show is muddee hear what are you going to get me for my birthday it is the 1 of may you need not get it till i get out there what i want you get me is a pony and saddle and bridle." The handwriting is crude, but the need is obvious. Perhaps it was the last time he could let anyone know about it.

After that, as far as I know, neither I nor anyone else knew what he needed. That wasn't the kind of question anyone asked at that period, especially of someone who looked like the man in the photo. I did have some idea of what he liked: good clothes, though he seldom bought anything but Pendleton shirts. Working on the twenty-six acres he and Mom had bought, making improvements like the pond he had dug to water his livestock and provide fishing for his grandsons and filling in the ravine that led from Eleventh Street. Remaining friends, mostly old drunks and old former drunks like Bill Robinson, a retired barber and longtime AA sponsor who gave up on Dad and probably gave him the bottle of untouched Lucky Tiger hair tonic that sat on top of his toilet tank.

Dad died in 1988, but odd things besides the photo remind me of him. Last year I got a call from an insurance company trying to track down policy holders. I told them I had no knowledge of ever holding a policy with them, but all the facts and the many addresses in their records checked out. Dad had taken it out in 1939, when I was five years old. Now it was worth four times the original benefit value. (My broker told me that the comparable figure today would be in the mid five figures.) Dad would have been pleased, and I was touched that in his way he was still taking care of me. And I had another view of him, this time of what he must have been like at thirty-one, less than half my current age, in a new and precarious business in a new town not all that friendly to outsiders.

I never talked to him about values, only listened to him about conduct—mine, mostly bad—but as I wrote a few years after his death in a book about Westerns, I came to realize what, at his best, he stood for: Tell the truth; pay your debts; meet your obligations; work hard; if it isn't working, try something else; take care of yourself and take responsibility for yourself; don't break down; don't blame anyone else for what happens; don't get beat by avoidable ignorance or weakness; stand by your own; don't whine.

A friend who read a draft of this piece said that she didn't get a clear picture of my father—that there seemed to all kinds of contradictions. As I said to Dad earlier about the photo, I'm just recording impressions. What he did may not add up to what he was, but I suspect that's true of most of us. He wasn't a great man and at times not even a good man. But his children and now his grandchildren have been the most stable and in conventional terms the most successful in the extended family, so he must have done some things right.

Anyway, I hope that my ex-wife was correct and that I do grow more like him, at least at his best. And I wonder what kind of father I have been. Probably in some ways better, in some not, though it's impossible for me to tell and in any case not for me to say. But as the insurance policy helped me to realize, the job is never finished.

BACK ROADS

The doctrine of Manifest Destiny presupposes constant movement westward to occupy new territory and find new opportunities, and in the early years of the twentieth century both sets of my grandparents came to southern Kansas to start new lives. My father's father came from Alabama to work on the Santa Fe Railroad; my mother's father moved from Evansville, Indiana, to become, off and on, a merchant and sometimes a public official. My parents met in Arkansas City, though by the time they married they had moved to Kansas City to work.

For a while, they returned to Kansas, and I was born in Lyons at the end of the trail that Coronado had traced from Mexico through the Southwest in search of fabled cities of gold. Not long after my birth, my parents followed my maternal grandparents on an extension of his trajectory east, settling some fifty miles from the head of the Santa Fe Trail, moved not by greed but by the need to find a refuge from the depression. Unlike Steinbeck's Okies, they headed east, winding up on separate farms in the Ozark foothills in Missouri.

Apparently they chose southwest Cooper and north Morgan County in order to circle the wagons. My mother's brother Bob and his wife had a chicken ranch near Otterville, though why and how they chose that occupation and location I never thought to ask. He had lost an arm in a car accident while working in the oil fields in

Aruba, but all his life he seemed to be successful in a series of businesses ranging from Otterville to Stockton, California.

Despite economic setbacks in the depression, my grandfather seemed able to bounce back in any number of jobs, and he settled into life and Republican politics in Morgan County and in 1936 was elected to the first of two terms as state representative. Had it not been for the Second World War, he would probably have stayed in Missouri and perhaps in office, but he returned to Evansville to work in a war plant building P-47 Thunderbolt fighter planes.

My family didn't stay on the farm any longer than my mother could help. In later life, my father seemed to enjoy the idea of farming, and he was not given to extended reminiscences. But once, talking about the rough times and people near Cole Camp, Missouri, where he clearly had felt at home, he added, "But then your mother got to chewing on me, so I went to Coffeyville (Kansas) and got a job selling lessons door to door." We never found out what the lessons were, and soon we were back in Arkansas City long enough for me to remember the last move, back to Missouri, in 1939. There my family stayed, and Grandpa and Grandma Murray moved there a few years after the war.

Except for Uncle Bob, who wound up dying in Rogers, Arkansas, after leaving Stockton, Otterville again, and Chanute, Kansas, none of those two generations ever moved back. (Dad did return to Arkansas City for his fiftieth high school reunion and came back the next day. Asked why he didn't stay, he said, "Aw, there was nothing but a lot of old sons of bitches!")

All that remains of those years are some yellowing photographs and a few of my memories, sharp in fragmentary detail but blurred at the edges. The stories, however garbled, are much clearer. But no matter where my family went, southern Kansas and especially Arkansas City was the center of family myth. Grandpa Murray's best stories, and Mom's stories about him, centered on characters he described or modified freely from Cowley County. Stories about my mother and father and Uncle Bob proved that they had not only been young but interesting, even adventurous, even more adept at getting into trouble than I could ever aspire to.

However, I am the only one of my siblings to leave Boonville, heading north and east and all the way to the Pacific before settling in Oklahoma, a few hours' drive from Arkansas City. But the only time I'd even been through there was to visit my uncle's widow, Aunt Goldie, in Sedan, Kansas, and then to meet my siblings for her funeral.

When I return to Boonville, once or twice a year, I don't take the route my parents and grandparents used and wouldn't even if I knew it, since at the start of any new trip I'm eager to get where I'm headed. Instead, I always go the same way, up Interstate 35 to Kansas City, then Interstate 70 to Boonville. That takes eight hours and a bit, depending on my mood and the traffic.

For the trip home, the fastest route seems less attractive. The ninety miles or so between Kansas City and Emporia can't, objectively speaking, be any duller than the drive northeastward, but, lacking the excitement of the trip out, it seems three times as long. The other major route heads south from I-70 on U.S. 65, on the fringe of the Ozarks but mostly prairies, to pick up I-44 at Springfield all the way to Oklahoma City, and that was once rated as one of the leading boring drives in America. And it's only ten miles or so shorter than going through Kansas City and takes you through Tulsa, which jams every truck going east and west onto the Skelly freeway.

If I have time and patience, I've sometimes back-roaded along state and national highways, jogging left and right from one to another. Once I even tried going around Branson (motto: "You thought our stars were dead") by way of Fort Smith, Arkansas, but that is a very long drive, and except for the pool hall that Uncle Bob left when he died in Rogers, I have no memories or any other associations with that state. But mostly I've gone the shortest way possible, though that isn't very short.

The last time I headed south and west, I couldn't make up my mind. My sister Beth travels a lot on business, and a colleague once asked if she ever drove on a highway that had numbers, as opposed to lettered county roads. She recommended a route so complicated that her husband said it made him dizzy just hearing about it.

It wasn't until I got to the on-ramp to I-70 that I made up my mind to take the longer route. I'd made a leisurely drive to a meeting in Omaha on the way up, using back roads, and that had been enjoyable. So I was going to take Cooper County Route B to Missouri Highways 5, 52, and 53 to U.S. 54, as Beth had suggested. Then I was on my own.

But when B jogged south, I had the urge to continue on County J through Bunceton to see what a place where I'd played basketball looked like—pretty much derelict, as it turned out—and then over to 5 north and west of where Beth had suggested and west on U.S. 50, which now bypasses Otterville. I had stopped there on another trip, and I had driven through it with my brother when he was inspecting road work during a term as county commissioner, so I had no urge to return.

But I was drawn to Florence, Missouri. I had passed through there and had even taken a photo of the now deserted store that my grandfather had run in the now mostly deserted hamlet. The place is unincorporated, and it was never very large. So I wasn't hopeful about finding anyone. But there is a general store—that and the post office the only buildings open—so I stopped for coffee and perhaps information.

Told about my grandfather's store, the pleasant fortyish woman pointed to a ruddy, stout (in both literal and colloquial senses) elderly farmer and said, "He might know something about him."

Mr. Hurky (phonetic spelling) certainly did. He had hauled water to my grandfather's farm with horses, and he gave directions to the farm. My grandfather always smoked a crooked pipe, which was more or less true. He once bought a horse from Hurky's mother, who had warned Grandpa that the horse was hard to catch. "I can take care of that," Grandpa said, and he did. Hurky assumed that he gave the horse sugar. He remembered that Grandpa had been something in Jeff City and tentatively identified the house where Grandpa and Grandma had lived and which I had just seen in a photo in a box-full my sister keeps.

None of this was earth-shattering, and it didn't really tell me anything I didn't know about Grandpa, but it pleased me to learn that someone else had known, from another angle, the man who had taught me so much about how to do things and, more important, how to look at the world.

Partly as a result of this stop, I had the urge to look into a place in my father's past. Cole Camp, with a population just over 1,000, looked huge compared to the country I had just driven through, and it had a commercial district that stretched two blocks on either side of Highway 52 and seemed to have actual businesses. Partly out of filial piety and partly out of hunger, I drove up the main street and found a bakery. The born-again (and very competent) baker would not have found my father good company, but he and his wife could talk to me about their plans to be writers after they finished talking with a woman working on a master's degree in aviation safety— clearly, in October, 2001, a growth industry.

Then, skirting Warsaw and some of the oldest resorts on the tail of the Lake of the Ozarks, I drove through hamlets a lot like Florence, to El Dorado Springs and its faded spa to join U.S. 54.

I don't know how my grandparents got to that part of the country, but even now the main route to Kansas from Missouri south of Interstate 70 is U.S. 54, which we took on rare trips to Wichita to visit the family of Dad's estranged brother. There are a number of ways to go south and west from Fort Scott, or rather first one direction and the other. I chose to go to Girard in homage to the Little Blue Books that purveyed cheap information and attitudes in the 1920s and later, and then over Kansas Highway 57, so broad and well-maintained that some politician with a lot of clout must live in the area.

By this time I was conscious of backtracking through my family's past, and I headed for the first time to Parsons because it had been the end of Dad's run in the Missouri, Kansas, and Texas Railroad during World War II. The Katy is gone, subsumed, like its rival in Boonville, the Missouri Pacific, into the Union Pacific system. But Parsons has some handsome Victorian buildings and, just observable over the rooftops and raised right-of-way, the pseudo-gothic spire of the railway station.

I didn't linger in Parsons or try to find the railroad yards because in more than fifty years anything my father might have seen would almost certainly be gone. Besides, even if I could find out, I wasn't sure that I wanted to know where he had been. Probably he headed for a beer joint, and that was the best scenario. In some late-night diatribes, Mom accused him of "trashing around," how justly I never knew. He was a handsome man, and railroad division points are not always bastions of purity. In any case, finding an equivalent to Mr. Hurky was improbable, since Dad was in and out of there only between 1942 and 1945 and interacting with other transients.

So out of Parsons with an unsatisfiable curiosity about Dad's grown-up life away from home and kids, and down into the south end of the Flint Hills, few trees and lots of stone. A brief glance at Sedan because I couldn't remember where my aunt had lived—somewhere east of downtown, south of the main street, now the business route of U.S. 166—and past Cedarvale, where she was raised. In some ways, I knew her better than I did my uncle, but I realize that I didn't really know her at all. Besides, there were no family stories about her—you have to be a blood relative with a long and preferably disgraceful history to have a place in that episodic saga.

Arkansas City is the epicenter of those tales, but I wasn't old enough when we lived there to have any landmarks except Summit Street, down which some unspecified ruffians, probably including Dad and Uncle Bob, had rolled the streetcar into a canal. I didn't know where the school principal's house had been to which Uncle Bob had gone to pelt with rotten eggs. On the way, he tripped and came home with his sweater soaked.

I didn't even try to look for the house where Dad's half-sister Nanelou had lived. She took charge of me in the summer of 1939 when Mom was pregnant with my brother John, but we stayed there only a little while before going to New Mexico, still exotic in my imagination.

Nor could I remember the location of the house on the dusty street from which we made the final move to Missouri. Or that of the second-floor apartment where we had lived before the first move, though it was near a movie theater, probably on Summit, while my parents ran the Silk Hat Café. I called it the "sick cat," and once, taken by my Aunt Nanelou to the Presbyterian church north of Summit, still there, I scandalized the congregation by standing up in the pew and saying, "Let's go to the Sick Cat and get a beer!"

I forgot to look for the theater next to the café where I have my first memory of seeing a movie. I was taken in midway through a prison film starring James Cagney, and as we walked down the aisle, he was walking toward the camera with a very grim look on his face. I didn't know anything about aesthetic distance, and I turned and fled.

Arkansas City still has a daily newspaper, the *Traveler*, and it needs a reporter and feature writer. For a moment I was tempted to apply, mostly because that would give me a chance to go through the microfilm files to find out what my grandfather really did to get the natural gas supply restored. And when. That, and the search for other landmarks, is for another trip.

The Cherokee Strip Museum, commemorating the start of the 1889 Land Run, was closed, and anyway, that event played no part in the family story. Mom did tell the story of a large basketball player from Chilocco Indian School who landed in her lap while she sat in the front row cheering on Ark City.

Crossing the border into Oklahoma occasioned little emotion. Though I have lived in Oklahoma more than twice as long as I lived in Missouri, I have never learned to regard myself as an Oklahoman. Still, the sight of bright green winter wheat, the first crops in the journey, did lift my spirits.

Then Ponca City, the party town for Ark City young people, as, for younger Ponca Citians, Ark City was by the 1950s. Ponca City is on the border of my personal story as an adult, and the rest of the trip brought memories only of trips to swimming meets with my children.

Those are less deep and less poignant than memories of my own generation and of our predecessors, and even less vivid than my memories of traveling on my own, being my own person, after the family disintegrated and before my children and I were able to approach each other as adults.

Now I wonder if my children, who moved from the Gulf of Mexico to the far Southwest and from the Hudson River almost as far as the continent reaches, have anything like my sense of and connection to the past. They were less connected with grandparents, uncles, aunts, and cousins than I have been, and they don't remember the only big move they made, from California to Oklahoma. Perhaps they can't feel the way I do about the family past. Or perhaps they aren't yet old enough for it to matter.

TULSA TIME

How you feel about coming to Oklahoma depends on the time of year and the direction. Approached from the Texas Panhandle, Oklahoma seems positively verdant, giving the first view of cultivated ground since . . . since you left Oklahoma headed west, come to think of it. But coming from the east, through the foothills of the Ozarks, Oklahoma looks like what old geography books called The Great American Desert.

Except in winter and late spring. My first trip to Oklahoma as an adult was on Holy Saturday in the early 1960s. I'd left winter in Chicago and driven into late spring, and at Easter Mass in Norman I was struck not only by the contrast between the tanned and healthy-looking natives and the pasty winter complexions I was accustomed to but also by the church building, which looked more like a simple New England church than like the large and ornate pseudo-Gothic structures in the Chicago diocese.

The only really impressive structure in town was the football stadium (now considerably higher than it was then)—where the heart is, there will your treasure be also. Bobby Bare, who recorded "Drop Kick Me Jesus Through the Goal Posts of Life," may have been born in Ohio, but he's an Oklahoman in spirit.

At that time, I had no idea that I would spend half my life in Norman (cynically called "Normal" by disaffected residents). But in 1967, my job in California dried up and blew away, and, a reverse

47

Okie, I headed east, driving in a Pontiac listening to "California Dreaming" until I lost it at San Bernardino, got ripped off in true *Grapes of Wrath* fashion by a service station attendant in Seligman, Arizona, and in Oklahoma City was blocked by a local purposely straddling the lane lines on the freeway.

When I got settled, I discovered that the neighbor across the street was from Ventura and the one around the corner was from Santa Barbara. We would stand around complaining about how low taxes were because you certainly don't get what you don't pay for.

Early on, I saw an editorial in the *Daily Oklahoman* (according to the Columbia School of Journalism the worst metropolitan newspaper in the United States) opposing government giveaways, and I wondered if the very aged publisher and founder remembered how the Territory was settled. He should have; he'd practically been there.

My grandfather, who did remember, had been an official in Cowley County, Kansas—the startline for the 1889 Land Run—and he had always spoken scornfully of the natives, by which he did not mean Indians. "Sooner? Sooner steal than work!" I thought he was, characteristically, exaggerating until I read the editorial and realized that the University of Oklahoma fight song, "Boomer Sooner," not only celebrated those who beat the gun to steal land but that the song itself had been lifted from Yale's "Boola Boola."

My first students were easier to deal with than the very bright but sometimes semizonked surfers in Santa Barbara, and I was stuck by their diffidence about their native state. Although they were too polite to come right out and ask what I had done to get sent to Oklahoma, they clearly wondered. And when, in a discussion of Restoration London, I said that every age has a vision of where the real action is—Italy in the English Renaissance, Paris in the 1920s, and so on—and asked them the comparable location in Oklahoma, they said, sheepishly, "Norman."

Later, every time I taught *Adventures of Huckleberry Finn*, I would read the closing lines about lighting out for the territory in order to escape from female-dominated respectability and ask the students where Huck was going. First blank looks, then dawning comprehension, then horror at the difference between Huck's dream and the reality they saw, in Okieism, "Rat cheer."

Their diffidence was rather charming, certainly more palatable than the obverse attitude I ran across at a conference banquet at Panhandle A&M College (now Panhandle State University). The woman seated next to me said, with great self-satisfaction, that some students had come from New York City to learn how real people lived. When I suggested a mutual exchange to show Oklahomans the outside world, she clearly had no idea what I was talking about.

Later, at another kind of banquet I wouldn't ordinarily go to, another woman asked where I was from. "Norman," I said.

"Oh," she said, obviously enlightened, "you're not a real Oklahoman, are you?"

I should have used the Flannery O'Connor's response to the question "Are you saved?" "If you are, I wouldn't want to be." Or "Better later than Sooner." But I didn't think of either, which is probably just as well.

Of course, the woman was right. When I saw some of my books in a library exhibit of Oklahoma authors, I said, inwardly, "No!" And once I was free to travel more or less at will, I spent every summer out of the state for twenty years. In fact, that's pretty Oklahoman, since natives seem to believe that if they live right, they'll go to Santa Fe when they die.

Actually, there is a lot to like about Oklahoma and Oklahomans. The two women were exceptions to the high standards of politeness and openness of the people. They are good at making fun of themselves, even of the state inferiority complex. Not a real Oklahoman, when confronted by an easterner making fun of them, I placed my hand over her face and gently pushed.

And I grew to enjoy the scenery of the state, which is varied if undramatic, and I became patriotic enough to resent outlanders laughing at Mount Scott, which reaches 2,464 feet above sea level. May is lovely, if you don't count the tornados, which long-term residents don't, and October is as perfect as weather can get.

When I decided to move away, there was almost nothing about institutional Oklahoma that I regretted leaving. The congressional delegation is so unspeakable that the loss of a House seat after the 2000 census was a blow for democracy. The university had become wealthier but meaner, and instead of naming buildings for faculty who had served long and well, the current practice is to sell naming rights to the highest bidder. The *Daily Oklahoman* is terrible, but the Norman newspaper seems to have the motto "See no evil, hear no evil, speak no evil." Politicians seem to think that if they only cut taxes and gut unions, Oklahoma will become a mecca for business, OU will never again lose to the University of Texas, and closet Republicans can go on pretending they are Democrats. Even more depressing, they keep getting elected on this platform.

But not long before I left, I drove east of Norman into the edge of the Cross Timbers country and realized that I will miss the red dirt and the rolling prairies and even the stubby oak trees. The skies. The sunsets. More people than I realized. Some unique Okie expressions like "right-at figure" for a rough estimate.

However, as my departure date neared, my chief anxiety about leaving was that I might not be able to. A typical late-January storm was predicted the day the movers were to load my furniture, and as that day approached, freezing rain iced in roads and downed trees and power lines farther and farther south in the state, giving me still another reason to leave. If I could.

But apparently God dropped everything else, and though the night before I loaded thunder and heavy rain kept me awake, the freeze line stopped about eight miles north of Norman. Willie, the very large and genial black man about my age who drove the van, had come up from Dallas and reported that road conditions were fine. He and his crew had me loaded before two o'clock, and I was free to turn in the keys to my apartment, say goodbye to the few friends who had not retired or moved away or both, and get ready for a thousand-mile drive the next day.

Next morning I was on the road by six, and again it looked as though I might not get out of a state I was more than ready to leave. At the end of the spur that connects to the H. E. Bailey Turnpike, I threw my quarters in the change basket and waited for the light to turn green. Nothing. No booth with an attendant. Red light and threat of a three-figure fine for running it.

Thank God for cell phones. A voice at the central office gave me the okay to proceed.

Farther down the turnpike, after daybreak, a line of electric company repair trucks headed north to deal with power outages that lasted as much as three weeks. Nothing much in the landscape, except for some good memories of the Wichita Mountains Wildlife Refuge, gave me any occasion for regret.

Of course, nothing for some five hundred miles promised anything better in the way of topography. The breaks leading up to the Llano Estacado east of Lubbock are the only feature to vary the monotony until you leave the plains for the valley leading up to Ruidoso and the spur of the Rockies.

Being in New Mexico always makes me feel better, even if I'm passing through, because I've done a psychological as well as literal time shift and am really west, where most of the place names are Spanish. Of course, radio reception pretty well goes to hell, but there's always AM, and just after sunset, west of Las Cruces, I hit the search button and got . . . KOMA, in Oklahoma City, 50,000 watts of clear-channel broadcasting, playing the Golden Oldies that had brought me to Oklahoma in the 1960s. It carried me into Lordsburg, and next morning, until the sun was over the low range of mountains to the east of Tucson, and then faded as smaller sundowner stations took over. I had never listened to KOMA while officially an Okie, and I was too old when I first heard the music to be nostalgic about it. But oddly enough, I missed the link.

Or did for about fifteen miles and began anticipating arrival at a new house, a new town, a new life, new FM stations with NPR and classical music and other features missing for most of the thousand miles.

For the next month, although I talked to several people in Oklahoma, the only time I thought about the state was when, every morning, I checked the weather page in the local paper and, like thousands of other emigrants, thanked God for the clear blue skies and balmy temperatures, lows in the 40s, which I was too new to complain about.

But when I went to a couple of Indian art fairs, an odd thing happened. I found myself gravitating to booths run by Cherokees, Muscogees, and Poncas, asking where they were from in Oklahoma, talking about a young Muscogee-Cherokee novelist whom I know and whose book I'd just reviewed, telling my companion, while watching a Kiowa dance group with a boisterous emcee, that Kiowas are like that. I acted as though they were homies.

That's odd. I'm the only poet to live more than thirty years in Oklahoma who doesn't claim to have Indian blood, not even from a Cherokee princess eight generations back, even though I have very high cheekbones. I'm not even a Wannabe, the largest tribe in America. I know and accept my heritage, which is terminally white and north European. I don't miss anything about white Oklahoma, and except compared to most other whites, I know very little about the cultures of the nations who live there except to call them nations, not tribes, and Indians, the term they use instead of the politically correct "Native American."

I can still get KOMA on my car radio after dark, and I still gravitate to artists from the Oklahoma-based nations at art fairs. So despite the fact that I am not, never was, and never will be a real Oklahoman, the memories I have are like a cord stretching a thousand miles that I cannot break.

ON THE ROAD

THE WORLD OF STEINBECK'S JOADS

Just over a hundred years ago, people waited in covered wagons and on horses for the signal to begin the Oklahoma Land Run of 1889 and get a new start on free land. Fifty years later, John Steinbeck's *The Grapes of Wrath* chronicled the beginning of the Joad family's trip west from Sallisaw, Oklahoma, out of an exhausted land, hoping for another new start in California. These images of Oklahoma dominate the popular imagination—and neither has anything to do, geographically or historically, with eastern Oklahoma.

Steinbeck is so closely identified with Oklahoma that for years even scholars believed, apparently from internal evidence in the novel, that he had come to Oklahoma to travel west with the Okies. Jackson R. Benson, his first real biographer, actually traced his movements and discovered that he had driven across the state on U.S. 66, well north of the Joads' route until Oklahoma City, but did no special research. He did travel with migrant Okies, but only in California.

Some Oklahomans were aware that Steinbeck knew absolutely nothing about the Sallisaw area, but even they concentrated on the general picture of the collapse of tenant and small farming and the destruction of a whole class of people and a way of life. And those who did notice seem, from Martin Shockley's account in "The Reception of *The Grapes of Wrath* in Oklahoma" (*American Literature* 14 [1944], 351–61), to have used his errors in description as an excuse for rejecting his real point. In fact, the official position in Oklahoma was that big capital was benevolent, Oklahoma's agricultural workers were among the most fortunate in the country, there were no Joads, and all was for the best . . . considering.

Since no Steinbeck critic seems to have bothered to check on the site of the first two hundred pages of the novel, I decided to make the journey to eastern Oklahoma to see what Steinbeck had missed and to get a sense of what he had been able to infer about the land and the people from the Oklahomans he had met in the California fields. What I found, not on any map or in any photograph I took, but there, between the lines of the novel where even Steinbeck could not have suspected it, was a piece of my own past and the past I share with my forbears and some of my contemporaries but not with my children. In fact, I am part of the last generation likely to read or read about the novel for whom it is not purely historical and scarcely credible.

Granted, my parents were not migrants, though they were certainly mobile during the depression years. But I was born in the middle of the Dust Bowl. My family lived for a while in Coffeyville, Kansas, about sixty miles west of Galena, starting point for the Wilsons who accompany the Joads from Bethany, Oklahoma, to Needles, California. My grandparents and later my parents hid out from the depression on hardscrabble farms in Morgan County, Missouri, back far enough in the woods that, like Winthrop and Ruthie Joad, I encountered my first flush toilet with deep suspicion. And my father had a good deal in common with Tom Joad, including his suspicion of government and his attachment to family, besides their age.

Furthermore, while I am not, to Oklahomans, an Oklahoman, my roots are in the region, and to bicoastal types and Yankees of all descriptions, including my colleagues, I apparently sound, look, and act like their stylized conception of an Okie. So I had some idea how it feels—and an even clearer idea after my journey through the countryside and through the novel.

At the beginning of the trip, however, I was only interested in tracing the route of the Joads. In outline, the geography of the first part of the novel is fairly simple: the narrative begins with Tom Joad near the end of his journey from McAlester State Prison northeast to the farm where his family live as tenants. The land is so flat that a truck travels a mile to the first turn and the "distance towards the horizon was tan with invisibility" (*The Grapes of Wrath*, Viking Critical Library edition, ed. Peter Lisca, p. 37). The dirt and dust are red; the land is under intense cultivation except where it is "going back to sparse brush" (37).

Uncle John's farm is near a highway (U.S. 59?) roughly twenty miles west of the Arkansas border, less than a day's journey by horse-drawn wagon going "the back way through Cowlington" (112). Thus the Joads live in northwest Le Flore County or northeast Haskell County, south of the Arkansas River, which forms the southern boundary of Sequoyah County, of which Sallisaw is the county seat.

In fact, though Steinbeck probably did not know and certainly, concerned with the plight of what he clearly thought of as real (i.e., white) Americans, did not care, the Arkansas was not only the boundary between the Choctaw and Cherokee Nations when this was Indian Territory, but it was one route for the Trail of Tears that brought the Five Civilized Tribes to the region after an upheaval at least comparable to the Joads' displacement by dust and tractors. Eastern Oklahoma is no longer Indian Territory, and in fact some whites settled there by relatively peaceful means before the Territory was subsumed into Oklahoma, but a lot of Indians still live there and they are very much present in the consciousness of Oklahomans. But the only Indian the Joads are aware of is the one pictured on the pillow which Grampa Joad has appropriated. In the minds of the generic tenant farmers in an intercalary chapter, they have a right to the land because "Grampa took up the land, and he had to kill the Indians and drive them away" (45).

When the Joads themselves are driven off the land—Steinbeck has no sense of history repeating itself—they begin their journey on a red dirt road until they reach Sallisaw, where they turn west on a concrete highway. From that point, and all the first day of the trip, Steinbeck gives precise mileage from town to town but almost no sense of the land on either side of the highway because both he and the Joads focus intently on the road ahead.

The exact measurement illustrates in reverse Ernest Hemingway's theory that a writer can leave things out if he really knows them. Anyone who travels the Joad route can see that Steinbeck hadn't the vaguest idea what the country was like but took refuge in very sharp close-ups of individual figures and in tableaux of groups, counting on readers as well as characters to focus "panoramically, seeing no detail, but . . . the whole land, the whole texture of the country at once" (145).

He was consistently wrong about what texture he gave. The land he purports to describe is in fact foothill country, the roads rising and falling, the horizons at most a mile or two away and always above eye level, the earth tan, the hills wooded, and the untended land soon choked with trees.

Of course, documentary precision has uncertain relationships to art, even to an art like Steinbeck's. And even had he been the most exact recorder of travels in the region, his novel would still be useless as a guide to the contemporary traveler. (Route 66, the Okie route to the Promised Land, has itself disappeared, subsumed into Interstate 44 east of Oklahoma City and into Interstate 40 westward.) Uncle John's farm would either be valuable lakefront property or at the bottom of Robert S. Kerr Lake. In fact, Oklahoma, its rivers dammed into lakes the shape of crab nebulae, now has more shoreline than Minnesota, and in eastern Oklahoma tourism and water sports are big business. As cause and by-product of all this water, modern Joads and landlords could ship their cotton via barge all the way to New Orleans on the Kerr-McClellan Arkansas River Navigation System.

But there is no cotton to ship. The bottom land shows no marks of cultivation except for occasional huge cylinders of hay too big for any man to lift, products of mechanization that will be applauded by anyone who has bucked eighty-pound bales six high on a flatbed truck in July. The land is, as Muley Graves says it should have remained, grazing land.

However, Steinbeck's Jeffersonian ideal of "a little piece of land" is not dead. Just south of Sallisaw and just north of "We Never Sleep Bail Bonds" is a billboard for "Wild Horse Estates / Want a Small Farm? / We Got Them"—two-and-a-half-acre tracts with running water, electricity, and telephone lines. But as the various trailer parks and RV sales lots indicate, Oklahomans are still on the move—if Dan's Mobile Home Repo Center or the adjacent cemetery don't get them first.

But once under the bridge that carries I-40 across Oklahoma, franchised America gives way to the world—if not the country—of the Joads. In Sallisaw, it becomes clear that Steinbeck did know something about the people of Oklahoma. A dark-haired man with an anxious look urges a battered yellow Japanese two-door along Cherokee Avenue, U.S. 64, and the main drag. A lean and ancient man—Grampa Joad buttoned up for Sunday—grabs a post supporting a metal sidewalk awning, his cane hooked over his free arm.

Scattered through town and all along the highway west are fossil records of the pre-interstate era, when two-lane concrete U.S. highways were state of the art. The buildings—mission-style garages, Bonnie-and-Clyde tourist cabins, mom and pop frame grocery stores, tumbledown gas stations stripped of hand pumps become chic decor—stand because no one needs the space they occupy and because it is cheaper to board them up than to demolish them.

The highways—U.S. 64 to Warner; U.S. 266 to Henryetta (Steinbeck spells it Henrietta); U.S. 62 to Oklahoma City—exist in a time warp. They aren't quite the Joad route: the old Hudson Super-Six traveled eighty-two miles from Sallisaw to Henryetta; today the trip is ten miles shorter. But essentially the road is the same: two lanes, no shoulders, the hard edge of the slab visible and dangerous, expansion joints whupping at the tires and jolting up through the backside every ten feet or so even in a modern car.

At Henryetta the Joads route disappears for nineteen miles into Interstate 40, and the modern traveler is forced to re-enter the late twentieth century. Here life is an accelerated version of what Steinbeck described in his intercalary chapters. The trucks are bigger, faster, and scarier than ever, and the drivers can no longer casually turn aside for a cup of coffee, a piece of pie, and a solitary flirtation with a fading waitress in a roadside diner; now they gather in flocks at enormous truck stops, which have everything a temporarily homeless man needs, including bunks, showers, electronic games, and sometimes assignations with hookers who conduct their business in aptly named recreational vehicles.

Some descendants of the Joads now travel the interstates. Ahead of me is a pickup truck bought, the little sign on the tailgate shows, in Blanchard, Oklahoma, loaded neatly, mattresses on edge lengthwise in the center, smaller pieces to either side, all roped snugly down. The driver, lean, weathered, and glum, his right hand atop the steering wheel with a cigarette sticking up between the index and middle fingers, might be, fifty years later, the reality of what Al Joad dreamed of becoming.

The man from Blanchard is too well off and not anxious enough to be a Joad. In fact, very few modern Joads use the interstate because their cars cannot maintain the pace. Occasionally you will overhaul a rusting, quivering, oversized American car of uncertain color and vintage, battered outside and tattered in, driven by an unshaven man with both hands firmly on the wheel, a shapeless wife beside him, and a bevy of tousled children staring from every window—open, in the summer, because the car never had air conditioning or it no longer works. If you think like a social scientist, you will agree with the Oklahoma sociologist, sympathetic in intention, who commented that

> The farm migrant as described in Steinbeck's *The Grapes of Wrath* . . . was the logical consequence of privation, insecurity, low income, inadequate standards of living, impoverishment in matters of education and cultural opportunities and a lack of spiritual satisfaction (Shockley, reprinted in Viking Critical Library edition, p. 682).

If you are an ordinary person, you will feel a moment's empathy for anyone condemned to that pace in that feeble a machine before thinking, in trucker's parlance, "I couldn't live like that." If you are in heavy traffic, you will curse the car and its inhabitants for clogging the flow of traffic and check the side mirror to be sure that no one is going to cowboy through by changing lanes right in front of you. But you are not likely to think that the inhabitants of the car are anything like you because if you did, or did for very long, you would not be able to stand the thought of someone living by standards of food, shelter, clothing, hygiene, and general quality of life that you could not endure.

One of Steinbeck's major accomplishments as a polemicist and as a novelist is that he presents us with a picture of a life that we could not endure lived by people whom we could not tolerate for a minute in everyday life and not only gives us no alternative to seeing them as human but makes us turn against our own kind and ourselves for turning away in distaste from a sleazy roadside diner or for driving too fast in new cars to avoid a dog on the road.

I didn't see any Joads on Interstate 40, but I did overtake a Mercedes 3000, driven well under the speed limit by a man dressed in camouflage fatigues and picking his nose. I assume that Steinbeck's waitress would label him a "shitheel."

That is an interesting term, undefined by Steinbeck but apparently referring in literal terms to someone so accustomed to indoor plumbing that, when forced to defecate in the woods, s/he is so unpracticed as to befoul the backs of the feet. Literally, if the fatigues were for use rather than fashion, the man in the Mercedes may not have deserved the label. But most of us would.

We would most especially deserve it in the connotative sense for equating humanity with a particular stage of domestic technology—or a regional accent or set of customs. The Joads, and to some extent these heirs of their dispossession, seem alien to us because they live in the way that country people had done for centuries before the rivers were dammed and the high lines brought Rural Electrification Administration power to light the houses and power the motors on the wells so that hand pumps could be replaced by indoor plumbing and before tanks of liquefied petroleum gas made wood gathering a recreation rather than a necessity.

That was not a comfortable life—it seemed, and was, a long way to the outhouse on a winter night, and even a chamber pot chills quickly after the fire dies. A coal oil lamp doesn't give off much light or a wood stove much heat, and you have to keep thinking about both in ways that even modern farmers cannot imagine. But in fact that life wasn't as hard to live as it is to imagine because country people had always lived that way. It was the culture they knew, material and otherwise, and they knew how to use it.

We don't, which is what makes us shitheels in varying degrees. But not very far beneath the surface, all of us Oklahomans—the sour man in the Chevy half-ton, the nose-picker in the Mercedes, and me in my stockpiled vita and '81 Honda—are Okies to somebody because of the way we talk or where we live or what we do and how we do it. To the sophisticated we are all quaint and irrelevant to what is really going on.

That morning I had left a motel whose marquee boasted, or

pleaded, "AMERICAN OWNED." The man from Blanchard carried a bumper sticker with the legend, "BUY AMERICAN GROWN, AMERICAN MADE—IT MATTERS." A four-wheeler's bumper announced, "HUNTERS FOR ENGLISH," though it probably referred to Congressman Glenn English (D-OK) rather than the movement to make English the official language, though the driver would probably support that too. Perhaps I should get a bumper sticker reading "HUMANISM: LOVE IT OR LEAVE IT" in response to new and alien critical technologies.

Like Muley Graves and the nameless tenant farmers in the intercalary chapters of *The Grapes of Wrath,* someone we don't know is doing something we don't understand and have no control over that is going to affect our lives in ways we don't even want to think about. We are going to have to change what we do or at least the way we do it, and at the same time, to preserve continuity and dignity, we must preserve a sense that what we did was coherent and valuable. The difference between us Okies, geographical and spiritual, and the rest of humanity is that we know it and resent it, asking in our various ways the question of the baffled tenant farmer: "Who do I shoot?"

The next question, less satisfying but more constructive, is "What do I do now?" The first step is to understand that there is a process and then to discover how to adapt to it, and if you are lucky or clever, to adapt it to one's tastes and abilities. The Joads begin by feeling the process and then discover the difficulty of adapting to a world in which their skills and values are irrelevant. That is what the first half of the novel is about, and Steinbeck understood and embodied this material very well. In the second half, the Joads begin to understand the process and to perceive the necessity of shifting from "I" to "we" and from clan to class. This sounds like whistling in the dark, though it is difficult to suggest a better way of building a kinder and more caring society. The last part of the novel presents the excruciating possibility that nothing can be done.

Despite the internal contradictions of this and most of his other novels, Steinbeck understood and presented extraordinarily well certain kinds of process, from the way a good mechanic fixes a car to the way a people adapt physically and socially to new situations. That makes almost all of his novels unusually readable paragraph by paragraph. More important, he could show the kinetic satisfaction and the cultural and spiritual value inherent in process, building characters and their world from the inside out. From the first, his novels also dealt with the necessity for human beings to adapt in order to survive. Because *The Grapes of Wrath* does so most thoroughly and most tellingly, readers all over the world have a clearer feeling not just for what it means to be an Oklahoman but what it means to be human.

STEINBECK AT THE ENDS
OF THE TRAIL

Reviled in his time, John Steinbeck turned out to be valuable, or at least useful, to towns at the opposite ends of the Okies' trail from eastern Oklahoma to the fertile valleys of California. Sallisaw and Salinas use him in quite different and probably incompatible ways. One is obviously, the other arguably, irrelevant to the vision that Steinbeck tried to embody in his best novels. The real moral of the two stories is what happens to a rebel who gets turned into a celebrity.

Even though Steinbeck never visited Sallisaw, Oklahoma, the town is the likeliest location of the town where the Joads and other tenant farmers go to get screwed by car dealers and bankers. However, since the early 1990s, Sallisaw has sponsored a "Grapes of Wrath Festival." That struck me and everyone I told about it as very strange.

After the novel was published in 1939, Steinbeck came in for a good deal of abuse. Guardians of the state's image tried to refute Steinbeck's image of the state. Some pointed out the indisputable fact that Steinbeck didn't know anything about the topography or crops of far eastern Oklahoma. But Steinbeck's portrait of dispossessed and desperate Okies presented a larger truth that has prevailed for more than half a century.

Later, apologists for the state tried to ignore Steinbeck or to put a positive spin on the word "Okie." One governor tried to rehabilitate it as an acronym for "Oklahoma Ingenuity and Energy" or something equally upbeat that no one believed for a minute or remembered for an hour. More memorable is Merle Haggard's claim to be "proud to be an Okie from Muskogee" (though he isn't, and when asked if he thought the town was really like that, he said no).

The Sallisaw festival apparently had a similar basis in public relations. At least the official tourism guide explains that "the Dust Bowl image of Oklahoma that John Steinbeck created in his famous novel 'The Grapes of Wrath' is laid to rest during the annual festival."

That sounded like a tall order for a two-day event, especially since Sallisaw was never in the Dust Bowl, and I was eager to see how the citizens of Sallisaw would go about it. I sent for information and got, in addition to reservation forms to reserve space to sell food, arts and crafts, and anything else, a list of festival activities. They included a 5K Run and, perhaps to take the curse off the European innovation, a two-mile fun run walk; arts and crafts; parade; antique car show; volleyball tournament; golf tournament; free entertainment; cruise night; and Ma Joad Chili Cook-Off. Except for the title and the last event, there didn't seem to be much about Steinbeck, or even dispelling the image he created, but perhaps it could be found in the atmosphere.

My impulse wasn't, or wasn't just, cultural snobbery. Sallisaw is the same size as my home town, I was born in the Dust Bowl, and I'm a reverse Okie. So I decided to go to see for myself.

It is possible to backtrack some of the Joads' route from Oklahoma City to Sallisaw along the old U.S. highways, but it is faster, simpler, and no less scenic to take Interstate 40. Either way, one is reminded of eastern Oklahoma's past as Indian Territory, at least in the exit signs like those for Wewoka, Wetumka, Weleetka. Casual ironies abound. Okemah, the home of Woody Guthrie, advertises an industrial park on a tee-and-golf-ball water tower. Checotah means "big chief," but billboards advertised the Cowboy Cafe and the Ranchhouse Restaurant.

Sallisaw is not far from the Arkansas border and just north of the Arkansas River, which divided the Cherokee Nation from the Choctaws. All but a few of the attractions listed in the Oklahoma guide, titled *Oklahoma Native America,* are associated with the tribe and its most famous member, Sequoyah, who devised the Cherokee alphabet.

Steinbeck didn't seem to know that the Sallisaw area had anything to do with Indians. Nor, as far as I could tell, did the sponsors of the Grapes of Wrath Festival, though it did turn out to have a Navajo Taco stand.

Near the interstate, Sallisaw could be almost anywhere, but on Cherokee, the main street where the Joads turned west on U.S. 64, the low buildings date from the twenties or even earlier, and the older residential area between downtown and the city park and rodeo grounds is positively bucolic: white frame houses, small, neat lawns, no sidewalks.

If I'd had any illusions of superiority, they would have been deflated when I missed the sign for the festival and headed north into the countryside past signs for Covenant Life Fellowship, Badger Lee Baptist, and Church of Jesus Christ, Sallisaw Restoration Branch. Jim Casy, Steinbeck's preacher who calls himself a Burning Busher, might have felt a little uncomfortable indoors, but before his conversion to transcendentalism, he would have felt at home theologically.

The parking area was more crowded than the grounds, but I found a place. The free entertainment, a very professional country band, was immediately evident. The members were dressed eclectically: fiddler in a cowboy hat, guitarist in a gimmie cap, string bass player in a bonnet and floor-length skirt (nothing weird; she was a woman), bareheaded women on banjo and fiddle.

Most of the exhibits in the "Antique and Specialty Car Show" didn't interest me much, partly because I don't like to think of models I have driven as being antique. But I was interested in the Steinbeck-era cars, including a 1930 Ford with a luggage rack and a 1926 Chevrolet soft-top, both restored, polished, and improved beyond recognition. Had the Joads' Hudson Super-Six made it through dust and flood, it would have blown away the competition.

Not all of the cars were rehabilitated. A man from Bokosha was asking $3,000 for a Plymouth contemporary with *The Grapes of Wrath*. The body had been sanded and primed, but the interior was beyond rough: upholstery leaked in several directions from the seat. Even more dilapidated were two body shells, without wheels or engines, sitting next to a table full of antique parts.

As I stopped to look at one car, a middle-aged and obviously rural couple standing next to it turned to me. They must have thought that anyone with glasses, a beard, and a camera bag would be an expert on just about anything. The man asked if I knew of anything that could get rust off a grill; the woman, if I knew where they could get a grill and a front fender for a 1961 Dodge. I pointed them to the men at the parts table and wished them luck.

By the time I got back to the stage area, the country band had given way to a group of children, identically costumed, tap dancing to taped music. With changes in costume, age, and levels of competence, group tap dancing continued throughout my stay. The groups drew most of the crowd—relatives, friends, or people starved for entertainment.

The booths in the craft area had a lot of space between them, and there were few patrons. The only things one hasn't seen a hundred times were a man chipping flint and some wooden constructions like wine racks with holes intended for two-liter plastic soda bottles.

I managed to avoid signing up for a free Bible ("Got one"), and I avoided two booths sponsored by the Republicans, one of them with the slogan "Get Right." There was no Democrat response. That would never have happened in Steinbeck's time or even before the past ten years. Of course, most Sequoyah County voters had been not Democrats but, like my father, Dixiecrats. Even so, he had been through the depression and remembered the legacy of the New Deal. The failure of historical memory—or perhaps the realization that his generation had passed and mine was passing—left a bad taste that was not cleansed even by an Emu Snack.

It was impossible to pass by the tables staffed by the emu people. I came away with seven separate items extolling feathers (for cleaning car bodies at GM), meat (fewer calories and less fat than any other creature with hide or feathers), and oil (the most remarkable cure-all since the stuff purveyed by medicine shows I used to see as a child), and praising emu ranching as a sure-fire route to a 30 percent return on investment. (Results may vary, as the ads say. In fact, the emu business turned out to be Enron with feathers. There was no market for any of the products, and the birds eat like garbage disposals. Farmers in Texas were turning them loose to roam the countryside and terrorize the natives.)

The emu people were pleasant and enthusiastic. A woman said,

"I ate my first emu stick not long ago. It was *good*. Then I saw you had to take the paper cover off."

Who could resist a sales pitch like that? I bought a stick for $1.25. It can't be called fast food—I had to take a knife to the plastic covering, and if the woman hadn't mentioned the paper cover, I wouldn't have noticed it. It was impossible to remove cleanly. Fortunately, the emu stick ("Boneless Emu Meat, Salt, Corn Syrup Solids, Spices, Monosodium Glutamate") tasted pretty much the same either way: a lot of spicy overlay with nothing much underneath. To check it out, write to Birds of Paradise Product Co. in Lawton, Oklahoma, if it still exists.

The one overt reference to *The Grapes of Wrath* at the festival was the sign for "Ma Joad's Chili Cook-Off" beside the fenced-in playground area and one booth inside featuring "Dust Bowl Chilly," with attendants dressed in sunbonnets and long dresses. At the cashier's desk, a woman told me that they had only started the cook-off last year, when rain spoiled the event. We agreed that today was gorgeous, despite the brisk wind blowing from the direction of the Sallisaw Restoration Branch.

It was only 11 A.M., but I had eaten a light breakfast at 6, so I paid $2.50 and got a small disposable bowl, a spoon, a soft drink, a napkin, and a token with which to vote for the best chili of the dozen entries.

The drill was to go around the circle of contestants, get a ladle from each pot, try that, and move on to the next table. Tasters could either stand or sit at one of the greening concrete picnic tables under the tall trees. I chose the handiest table, near the swings, and was joined by some local connoisseurs. A blonde woman, who with the right costume could have gotten a job as an extra in John Ford's film, fed chili to her small child. When he remained upright without bursting into tears, I knew that this sample was not going to get my vote.

My table was a tough audience. One man kept asking my advice about what to try next—the beard again?—and was himself a reliable guide. In fact, all of the entries seemed a little wimpish. Some was bland, some too sweet, a couple rubbery or otherwise inedible. Flouting the depression commandment to waste not, want not, we threw those out. The chili made from emu meat ran about the middle of the pack. That spooned out by the man dressed as W. C. Fields wasn't any tangier than the rest. None cleared the sinuses, a crucial test for anyone who has spent much time in the Southwest.

The people who sat with me at the picnic table came closest to taking me back to Steinbeck's time. Despite the fact that I was obviously a stranger, come all the way from Norman, everyone spoke to me not only pleasantly but naturally. I grew up in a town with rural roots, so I didn't think this unusual until I thought about it later.

More startling was the corn bread incident. The emu people had given me a chunk to eat with their chili, and I found it too sweet for my taste. I noticed that the toddler wasn't eating the chili or anything else, so I asked his mother if I could give it to him. Not only didn't she snatch her child away from stranger danger, she was surprised that I bothered to ask her first. (I never saw him take a bite, but at least he had something to carry around.)

In theory, I could have gone around the chili circle as often as I wanted, but I went back only to the table of the man who represented neither a business nor an organization, only himself, to make sure that I was justified in casting my vote for old-fashioned individualism.

When I did that on my way out, I found a harried-looking man in a sponsor's sweatshirt and asked him what I could do next. He pointed to a row of garden tractors and said that the tractor pull would start soon. So would the volleyball tournament. The parade? The new Miss America was making a triumphal return to Marlow, about twelve miles east, and she had in effect stolen the parade. Cruise Night? That would take place on the main drag of Sallisaw that night.

Although I hadn't been cruising in that sense for more than forty years, the event didn't seem worth an overnight stay. So I went to the parking lot and found it easier to exit than to enter a couple of hours earlier. After some franchised corporate ice cream near the interstate to settle the chili, I headed west.

It's hard to say what the festival was about, except the desire of the local Chamber of Commerce to get people to come into Sallisaw between Labor Day and Thanksgiving when the local racetrack didn't have a racing date. But I didn't see any obvious signs of commercialization, and one exhibitor said that the event hadn't been promoted very hard.

The result, as far as I could see, was that some people got together to show off or look at cars, crafts, talents, and emus. That was harmless and even enjoyable. But I was sorry not to see the Dust Bowl image laid to rest in more aggressive fashion, even if Sallisaw was never in the Dust Bowl. White-bread middle Americans like me don't have much contact with our collective past beyond the reflex, unexamined pieties learned in homogenized history and civics classes. A chance to celebrate, commemorate, or even commiserate about the real past, confused and troubling though it may have been, had been missed.

In contrast to the Sallisaw Chamber of Commerce, the founders and supporters of the National Steinbeck Center in Salinas, California, take Steinbeck and his legacy very seriously indeed. Film clips, mementos, artifacts—including signature shot glasses, beer mugs, and coffee mugs as well as T-shirts with quotations—and, during the annual festival, dozens of people are scattered about the gleaming building at One Main Street, which backs onto the railroad tracks. August, 2001, when I arrived, was a year too early for the centennial of Steinbeck's birth, and attendance was not as large as anticipated. Not everyone who signed up for the barbecue came to it, and a dance and another event had been cancelled. I don't know how well subscribed the various pilgrimages to settings in Steinbeck's novels had been, but it seems to me that anyone who has to visit the ranch that inspired "The Red Pony" or, as the *Literary Traveler* promises, "feel the characters' hats from *Of Mice and Men*," has a seriously deficient imagination.

The same thing might be said about those who really need to see the various exhibits. Some of them remind his readers, or tell them for the first time, of the conditions he protested. But like most museums, this one was squeaky clean—-a condition foreign to the blood, sweat, oil, and dust that permeate Steinbeck's novels of the 1930s.

Monterey is even cleaner than the Steinbeck Center, though Cannery Row is cluttered with tourists and vendors who stream by the bust of Steinbeck and Doc's laboratory. Nothing of the flavor—-the canning factories having closed—remains to remind the visitor of what the young Steinbeck and his friends were like.

Back at the center, it was easy to believe that the motives of the founders of the center were pure and earnest, but looking at Market

Street, which dead-ends at One Main, I wondered about those of the city fathers because the center looked a lot like the first step in an urban renewal project that had not moved across Main. A large vacant lot and a bail bondsman's office were visible from the front entrance, and on the left roughly four of six commercial buildings were vacant and one was getting ready to close.

Thinking back to Sallisaw, I wondered where Steinbeck would have felt more comfortable—or which Steinbeck at what period. The one who moved to New York and hung out with the rich and famous and had to travel with a standard poodle (imagine the young Steinbeck with a poodle!) might have been gratified at the shrine erected to his memory by belatedly grateful townspeople. But it's easy to imagine the young Steinbeck grinning at the little boy clutching his slab of cornbread and smiling wryly at the inflated hopes of the emu people. Maybe staying for the moonlight cruise and helping to fix one of the old cars. Even having a beer or a shot from a glass that didn't even bear his signature.

KICKING 66

Driving west from Oklahoma, I followed the Joad route on my way to do stoop labor at the Motion Picture Academy Library in Beverly Hills. Of course, I wasn't on "the Mother Road," as John Steinbeck called it, but the series of interstate highways that replaced it. But numerous billboards vainly erected to lure me into towns bypassed by the interstate reminded me of "Historic Route 66." One pointed the way to the longest surviving stretch of the old highway, eighty-some miles in an irregular bow up through Seligman, Arizona, to Peach Springs, Valentine, and Hackberry and back down to Kingman.

I didn't want to stop anywhere near Seligman because thirty years earlier, when I was moving from California to Oklahoma, a gas station attendant on Route 66, the main drag, had scammed me into buying a new alternator at five o'clock on a Saturday afternoon. But the AAA TripTik warned that there were no services for another fifty miles; I wasn't sure that my bladder would hold out; and there wasn't a tree to step behind. So I pulled off at Exit 123 to a convenience store.

It seemed only polite to buy something, and since I didn't need any more fluid, I turned to the rack of postcards and found, in addition to shots of regional landmarks and fauna, one picturing the 1937 original of "Historic Route 66" and the "1978 revision." Grass grew in the cracks of the narrow, virtually shoulderless concrete strip

72

curving into the foreground. The second ran, broad and straight, over the hill at the top, clearly an improvement even though the solid yellow line signaled that it carried two-way traffic.

I bought the card, and in the hours across the desert until I hit Los Angeles County traffic south of Victorville, it worked in my mind like sand in an oyster around which personal and cultural memories gathered. But instead of a pearl, the result was a conviction that while the physical location of Route 66 had a good deal to recommend it, it was highly overrated as a mode of conveyance.

When I got back to Oklahoma, I joined the usual gathering of colleagues for lunch and mentioned that I was thinking of writing an attack on Route 66 nostalgia. A retired engineer, the eldest, asked, "Why? It was a lot better than what came before!" The architect, involved in historic preservation of vernacular architecture, objected that on the interstate you missed the marvelous buildings in the little towns strung along the old highway.

The fourth man, a native Californian who had made the trip dozens of times, objected emphatically to these views. "Talk to me before you write it!" he said. "I have dozens of stories about how awful it was." Then, without waiting for my response, he began a litany: rip-offs at gas stations, fraudulent Indian artifacts at tourist traps ("Try explaining to a kid that Taiwan is an Indian village!"), farm tractors leading miles of impatient travelers, and tension about meeting someone head-on at the top of every hill. We agreed that anyone nostalgic for Needles, California, before air conditioning was welcome to our share of the experience.

But clearly we are in the minority. I already owned one illustrated book about Route 66 and had heard of another. A few minutes at the computer turned up a dozen more, including a cookbook, in local libraries, and in late 2001, amazon.com listed fifty-four books. In August, 1995, three exhibits opened in Oklahoma, and Clinton, Oklahoma, has what is billed as the Route 66 Museum, featuring newsreels, home movies, Route 66 trivia games, and a drive-in theater exhibit showing episodes of the TV show *Route 66*. The museum and exhibits are perhaps a bit too sparkling, including the vintage truck billed as something the Joads might have driven, except that it's a Ford rather than Steinbeck's Hudson.

The United States, all eight states on the route, the Netherlands, Belgium, France, Italy, and Japan have associations to direct their members' attention to the memory of the old strip. A website from Belgium offers versions in Spanish, German, French, Italian, and Portuguese; another, in the Netherlands, adds Finnish and Romanian to those western European languages. Three periodicals are devoted to the highway: *The Route 66 World News* (Elk City, Oklahoma; quarterly), *The Heart of Route 66* (McLean, Texas; monthly), and the glossy *Route 66 Magazine* (quarterly), published, ahistorically, in Laughlin, Nevada. The last is filled with ads for tours, sights, memorabilia, and even a "Route 66 Living History Work Shop." The Oklahoma Department of Tourism featured on the cover of its 1995 Vacation Guide "Inside Tips From the Road by Best-Selling Author and Route 66 Expert Michael Wallis." My local public television station ran a documentary titled "Route 66: The Road That Built America," in one shot of which a Rolls Royce glides down the old highway in Arizona.

There are festivals all up and down the road, especially in 2001, the diamond jubilee of its inception. The largest was probably in Albuquerque, New Mexico. It lasted three days, was expected to draw 100,000 visitors, and bring in $20 million. The celebration spread across the map and calendar to smaller venues. There's an annual motorcycle tour in June. And judging from the increase in websites, the craze for Route 66, perhaps even more in Europe than in America, keeps growing.

Looking through and at these artifacts and symptoms to try to understand their popularity, I found a curious blend of sentiment and fact. Three books, accessible from well-known publishers, will satisfy the curiosity of all but the fanatic or the motorcyclist or those wanting mile-by-mile guides to the road and its attractions. The soberest view of the highway is given by Quinta Scott (black and white photos) and Susan Croce Kelly (text) in *Route 66: The Highway and Its People* (Oklahoma, 1988). Michael Wallis has color pictures and a romantically inflated text in *Route 66: The Mother Road* (St. Martin's, 1990). Tom Snyder, "Founder and Director, Route 66 Association," uses old AAA strip maps and an informal style to guide the traveler over what remains of the old road in *The Route 66 Traveler's Guide and Roadside Companion* (St. Martin's, 1990). (These have all been updated.)

Snyder distinguishes between tourists who rush and travelers who mosey, but almost from its beginning, the people who created and promoted Route 66 as "the Main Street of America" were less interested in moving people than in getting them to stop. True, the National U.S. 66 Association's charter boosted the highway as "the shortest and most direct route between the Great Lakes and the Pacific Coast, traversing as it does the prairies of Illinois, the scenic beauties of the Ozark Region, the lead and zinc section of the Joplin-Miami district, the oil fields of Oklahoma and the Texas Panhandle, the south foothills of the Rocky Mountains in New Mexico, the Grand Canyon area, Arizona and Southern California." (The Mojave Desert is not mentioned.) But most of the signs and wonders described and illustrated in the books feeding and feeding on the nostalgia trip—cut-rate souvenirs, live rattlesnakes, and whatever might be advertised as largest, smallest, or deepest, at least between the sign and the attraction—were designed to turn tourists into travelers.

And what the books don't say, at least prominently, is that most of the attractions and almost all of the souvenirs were fake, from the sleaze of the Ozarks, which is the direct ancestor of Stuckey's, to the cleansing edge of the Mojave. Snyder asks, "Can you really go home without a rubber tomahawk?" Not the people who bought them and patronized the snake pits and other tourist attractions.

Most of these have mercifully disappeared, except for the Nemadji pottery advertised in New Mexico but made in various *faux* Indian designs by a succession of white people in Minnesota, but you can find descriptions and pictures of them in Thomas Arthur Repp's *Route 66: The Empires of Amusement*. The purveyors of these artifacts have mostly been replaced by stores like the upscale Route 66 in Oklahoma City, which is not on the original route but is stocking memorabilia as fast as Jeanette, the manager, can find high-quality merchandise to complement the multicolored telephone decorated with hair and eyes. When I talked to her, she was waiting for a shipment of Route 66 watches. Scattered throughout the store—to draw people through it—are coffee mugs, some authentic-looking, shot glasses, baseball caps, road journals encased in recycled license plates, both individual and mass-produced road signs, and a tie with a Chicago to LA Route 66 map on it, held with a clasp in the form of a semi and trailer, and videos covering either the whole route (Wallis again) or just the Oklahoma part. There are also reproductions of period postcards and either a painting or a very garish postcard of the sign for the Palomino Motel on Lincoln Boulevard a mile or so west. The sign remains, somewhat battered, but the motel is gone, displacing the hookers, state legislators, and other riff-raff who once made it a home away from home. Jeanette didn't have a Route 66 telephone yet, but she had been trying to persuade the artist to switch from hair and spangles to a style more in keeping with the shop's name.

Those who can't get to Oklahoma City or the Welcome Center and Gift Shop at Rancho Cucamonga in California (looking for a new home) or Clinton can shop online at the Route 66 Museum website and find, among very much else, Route 66 antenna balls and fuzzy dice. The Australian website Route 66 will sell you bowling shirts, but they have nothing to do with the highway, nor does Web66: A K12 World Wide Web Project. But there are plenty of other sites for state and national associations, local museums, maps, photos, travelers' accounts, a weather report from major cities from Chicago to Santa Monica, and a mile-by-mile description of the road (route66.exmachina.net) that is a marvel of diligence and ingenuity.

This kind of nostalgia is harmless enough, I suppose. It helps you to forget the realities around you, at least for a while, and to cultivate the easy astonishment that people before you had lives and jobs and interests. But anyone who really cares for the West will take more satisfaction in seeing fake ghost towns, built to attract uncritical tourists too timid to search out the real thing, ironically deserted in their turn.

Snyder is an enthusiastic purveyor of the view that Route 66 is somehow more authentic than the interstates, maintaining that "life begins at the off-ramp." By life he means the people, and like most of his colleagues he laments the fact that the interstates bypassed the people and businesses that fed off Route 66. Michael Wallis, who traded "Forewords" with Snyder, pastoralizes the people who "sleep like babies" because they "find time holy" and are reassured by the knowledge that "the Mother Road is there." He also praises, in language even more sentimental than Steinbeck's in *The Grapes of Wrath*, "waitresses with coffee pots welded to their fists," a formulation that reduces the women to their functions. Perhaps he should have read another Steinbeck novel, *The Wayward Bus*, which gives a somewhat grittier view of the trade. And he should have consulted one of my colleagues, who remembers the Clinton, Oklahoma, radio station's noon broadcast of interviews with tourists at Uncle Corny's Restaurant (burned out in 2000), who provided a window on the outside world as well as news about road conditions and life in general, from a local café. This was in the days before the Oklahoma Route 66 Museum opened to instruct tourists rather than air their views. My friend didn't comment on the waitresses or, for that matter, the food. Perhaps she had blocked the memory.

Still, even in the most nostalgic of these books a glimmer of reality occasionally pierces the fog of disordered memory laid down by Wallis and his peers. First, it is obvious to a moderately careful reader that the "real people" extolled in the books are getting old. Many of them have been successful enough to raise children who don't want the family business, and in many cases the parents don't want them to. Over and over, small business owners say, with varying degrees of emotion, that the place will die with them. Some blame Lady Bird Johnson for taking away the billboards that brought them customers and littered the roadside. A few are philosophical enough to say, without rancor, that the road gave and the road took away.

The second historical reality, which even the most sentimental writer is forced to recognize, is that Route 66 itself disrupted previous patterns and, in various reroutings, left high and dry towns all the way from the Illinois corn fields to the California desert, including Santa Fe. Clines Corners, the rubber tomahawk capital of New Mexico, had to move three times to stay on the highway. This complication is recognized even by *Route 66 Magazine,* where an editorial seems to oppose a plan to restore the highway, asking "what parts of the road are to be preserved? Is it the original, late 1920s road? Is it the postwar 'so-much-traffic-we couldn't-cross-the-road' which bypassed many towns in Illinois, alignment? (In Arizona alone, three alignments of Route 66 exist literally side-by-side.) Who will decide which one to preserve, and why?" The writer concludes, though it isn't stated quite this way, that Route 66 should exist as a state of mind rather than a road.

Third, there is the sticky question of engineering. In an uncharacteristic moment of realism, Tom Snyder points out that "the innocent-looking little half curbs" that flared up at pavement's edge on one stretch in Oklahoma "could turn a hill face into a solid sheet of water during a hard rain" and tended, instead of guiding cars back on the highway, to flip them over. (My friend from Clinton remembered them vividly, without prompting from any printed source.)

Michael Wallis scorns details of highway engineering to assert that, unlike the interstates, "Route 66 honored the land" by following its contours rather than cutting straight ahead. This ignores the obvious facts that it did so because of technical and financial limitations and that if it had really honored the land, it wouldn't have been there at all. But even he is forced to admit that Route 66 was so dangerous that the owner of a wrecker service rejoiced when the interstate opened because he was tired of hauling bodies out of cars in head-on collisions.

By the time I had been through this material, the mild superiority to 66 nostalgia I had felt on the outskirts of Seligman had given way to irritation that was not so much unreasonable as unexplained.

I came up with two explanations, stylistic and historical. I objected to the title "The Road that Built America" because it is hyperbolic and not entirely accurate. It does symbolize what Steinbeck called in "The Leader of the People" the westering impulse of Americans and explains why, as the writer Frank Chin said, it may have been a two-way road, but it's a one-way myth. There are not songs about heading east from California on 66, and only one I can think of about leaving the west:

> *Fifty miles to water,*
> *A hundred miles to wood.*
> *To hell with this damned country,*
> *I'm going home for good.*

Lots of people did go back, of course, but most didn't, except the Rams NFL team, which came from Cleveland to Los Angeles and then headed back to St. Louis. Any longtime baseball fan can remember when the major leagues ended at St. Louis and the Pacific Coast League strove for equal status. Population and fashion shifted to the left coast, and Route 66 serves less as means of travel than as symbol.

In other words, the highway was important, but it wasn't all-important, even for the regions it traversed. But I have a chauvinistic reason for thinking Route 66 nostalgia intolerable. I grew up on U.S. 40, which ran from sea to shining sea, not just from Lake Michigan to the Pacific, and which, more important to me as a child, could take me from Boonville, Missouri, to the magic cities of Kansas City and St. Louis. But I did not mourn when Interstate 40, which replaced it, was pushed through several miles south of town.

Perhaps I didn't feel nostalgic about U.S. 40 because the first two decades of my life were strung along the Santa Fe Trail. I had been born near its middle, raised very near its beginning—the street name "Santa Fe Trail" was more than a developer's fancy—gone to college and graduate school at two points on it and worked in a town built around a fort constructed to protect its travelers. One of my aunts worked in Las Vegas, New Mexico, the last big stop before Santa Fe.

But despite the pleasure at being associated with history and my continued feeling that New Mexico is a natural destination, I have never had the urge to retrace the route or to venerate relics from it. The trail had served its purpose—getting people from one place to another. It was replaced for that purpose by other routes and means of transportation.

Another reason for resisting the 66 cult is that I have a very good memory, which makes it difficult to be nostalgic.

I made my first trip on Route 66 in 1952, from El Reno, Oklahoma, to Albuquerque, and I felt a thrill at heading west and seeing, at sunrise in eastern New Mexico, the first mountains I can really remember. And of course I knew Bobby Troup's "Get Your Kicks on Route 66," though I didn't know that his wife Cynthia had suggested the title, and felt some thrill at being on the actual road. But even then I saw that the highway was less a route for the traveler than a commercial enterprise, since the billboards were sleazy even by Highway 40 standards. And, I realized when I drove all the way to California in 1965, I hadn't seen the worst, the billboards in which rival sellers of Indian souvenirs alternated insults of each others' goods all the way across western New Mexico and eastern

Arizona. None of the nostalgia books contain photographs of these signs, perhaps because the politest of them said things—like, "Don't buy from Chief Kiss-My-Tokus"—that might make even a white bigot cringe today.

I can't be the only one to remember more conventional discomforts, like driving the interminable few blocks down the main streets of small towns not different enough from Boonville to justify the delay, even on a corner in Winslow, Arizona (which now uses the Eagles' line on a billboard), let alone Weatherford, Oklahoma. Or following a pickup loaded down with a camper and towing a boat up the 2,300-foot climb from Needles to Mountain Springs Summit in the Mojave Desert. And this on a two-lane road in 110-degree heat, chewing sand because, in the absence of air conditioning, the windows had to be rolled down.

I mentioned these details to Jeanette at the Route 66 store in Oklahoma City. She is too young to remember when cars weren't air-conditioned and two lanes were what you had, mostly, but, surrounded by reconstructed relics of the Mother Road, she shuddered at my description.

Michael Wallis laments the passing of restaurants where the person who served your pie had actually cooked it, assuming, apparently, that the person knew how to cook. He may be right, but I don't remember anything I ate on various trips along Route 66. Everything being compared to what, there is a lot to be said for McDonald's and the chain truck stops along I-40. They may not have Art Deco or semiauthentic weathered Western charm, but at least you know what you're going to get. And west of Needles, up the slope to Mountain Springs Summit, I-40 widens to three lanes to let me past semis, campers, and other obstacles.

Even if I accepted Tom Snyder's distinction between tourist and traveler, I have never put myself in either category. In 1952, and many times in recent years, I have paralleled the old 66 route, through the familiar, incomparable landscape, to reach people who are much realer to me than a waitress with a coffee pot. I'm pleased to be able to do it with less physical and aesthetic strain than I did over Route 66 thirty years ago.

In 1965 I drove to a job in California in a Pontiac Catalina with an uncomfortable bench seat and a 385-cubic-inch V-8 engine that got at best twenty miles to the gallon even without the burden of air conditioning. A year later, having sworn never to spend another night in Victorville, California, I drove straight through from Albuquerque to Santa Barbara and arrived, exhausted, just before midnight. (First I had to drive east, obviously, but remember, it's a one-way myth; the Mother Road runs west, and there is no California-to-Oklahoma nostalgia.) Thirty years later I rode comfortably in the bucket seat of an air-conditioned Plymouth Colt with half the cylinders and almost twice the gas mileage. Driving about the same distance, I arrived in Santa Monica in time for dinner.

What had I lost? Well, I hadn't been able to see downtown Needles again, but Needles is like a sigmoidoscope: sometimes essential, but never pleasant. A leisurely look at the landscape? In 1980, my children were as awed at the first sight of the New Mexico mountains and Tijeras Pass into Albuquerque as I had been in 1952. When I hit the pine forests near Flagstaff after miles of desert, the air smelled and tasted no different from I-40 than it had from Route 66. And I could spare far more attention to all of it at seventy miles an hour on I-40 than I could on Route 66 partly because, thanks to Lady Bird, most of the tasteless signs were gone but mostly because there was far less chance that some idiot was going to hit me head-on or pull out in front of me from a barely discernible side road. And I could take some consolation in the responses of Bobby and Cynthia Troup, who are responsible for so much of the hype. She thought it "just a long road with cheap motels and restaurants." He remembered it as "possibly the worst road I'd ever taken in my life."

I had to agree with these experts. So I don't plan to drive down Historic Route 66 and buy an alternator in Seligman. But I hope the gas station has one to fit the next Rolls Royce that takes the old road.

FLYING IN THE HEARTLAND

Basketball coach and raconteur Abe Lemons tells a story about his father's taking him on a train to see buffalo because one day there wouldn't be any more buffalo. Now, Lemons said, we're up to here in buffalo, but there aren't any more trains.

From 1999 to early 2002, that hasn't been quite true for Oklahomans, but funding for the Heartland Flyer and for the whole Amtrak system is precarious. Before the train disappeared, and while I still lived in a town with train service, I decided to take my first train ride in Oklahoma in thirty years.

Norman's station went into rehab just after I traveled, but on the Saturday I caught the train, a group from Passenger Rail Oklahoma (PRO) was using it to serve coffee and doughnuts and urge people to write state and national legislators not only to save the service but to extend it.

On that misty Saturday, the PRO people and their families outnumbered passengers, and there was plenty of room on board when the train arrived on time at 8:50 A.M., twenty-five minutes after leaving Oklahoma City.

The equipment is impressive even, as another traveler observed, by European standards—double-decker cars with reversible seats, large and gleaming bathrooms with plenty of paper and towels, a snack bar with prices that will astonish those used to buying food at airports: $.75 for milk, $3.75 for a double cheeseburger, and so on).

A conductor said that some businesspeople use time on the train to work on the way to Fort Worth, but that Saturday, for most of the passengers, the journey mattered more than the destination. It was a day for family excursions. About a dozen people got on at Pauls Valley, including Stormy, five and a half, and her grandparents, taking her to meet her mother after a Christmas visit. Stormy was taking her first train ride; so was her grandmother, who seemed a little less excited. They had driven over from a small town on U.S. 75 in order to catch the train. A father of two older children had bought tickets as a Christmas present for his family. They were going to the Stockyards and hoped to find some good Mexican food.

Except for the ride through Big Canyon (big by Oklahoma standards) along the Washita through the Wichita Mountains, where bald eagles dot the trees and the canyon walls and river are beautiful even in January and otherwise inaccessible at any time of year, you wouldn't take the train for the scenery.

What you do get is a look at Oklahoma's back yards, beyond the kind of thing that Michael Wallis waxes poetic about in his books and tapes on Route 66 and that you don't see from I-35. There are the industries that give towns a reason for being like the refinery at Wynnewood, the quarry at Crusher, something large but enigmatic at Ardmore. There are remnants of a time when the railroad was the major link: deserted warehouses and hotels; declining business districts on streets leading to what is now the real town.

Some surprises, like the sign at Gainesville "Limo Traffic Only." I didn't see any limos or hard evidence of promised public transportation, but another dozen people got on, one family with enough luggage to identify them as real travelers.

Closer to Fort Worth, more and more of the ugly urban infrastructure that makes all cities run. Finally the old Santa Fe station, which looks better on the inside than it does on the outside, only ten minutes late, having made up twenty minutes from Gainesville.

Then reality intrudes. At any major European station, the arriving passenger has a number of choices. In Budapest, for example, the three major stations have subway stations and numerous connections to streetcars and trolleys, not to speak of ranks of taxi drivers who practically come up the steps to grab your bags.

But at Fort Worth, if you aren't being met, you have to confront the issue of what you do then. If you don't plan to stay in Fort Worth, you can catch the Texas Eagle to San Antonio (and, after a six-hour wait for another train, to Los Angeles, at least three days a week) or to Chicago at the new Intermodal Center. If you want to go to Dallas or several places along the way, including D/FW, you can catch the Trinity Railway Express at the same station, but for the regular schedule, you have to wait three and a half hours.

If you're going to Fort Worth proper, you may have a problem—not with things to do, but with getting to them. On that Saturday, there were no taxis, and a businessman I talked to on the way back said there hadn't been any waiting on the weekday he arrived, though at the station they were happy to call one. The conductor said that trolley service from the station had been suspended because of low ridership, but the Tarrant County public transportation website promised trolley service to the Stockyards and to the museums in the cultural district, though it didn't say how often it ran or how much it cost, and the website was slow and not very informative.

Another problem is lack of promotion. Like many people, I vaguely knew about the Flyer, but it didn't really sink in until the ads for special trains to the University of Oklahoma's Cotton Bowl game with Arkansas appeared. Fort Worth attractions and Oklahoma travel agents could arrange excursions to special events, with hotel and transportation tie-ins. It would be harder for Oklahoma City and Norman to do so because the daily train from Fort Worth doesn't arrive until late evening. And it might not be worth their while, less because of numbers of passengers than because of the train's uncertain future—still another example of a day late and a dollar short.

That future, or lack of it, raises concerns in cities that have put or are putting money into their stations. Purcell has a new depot; Norman is restoring its historic depot. If funding does not continue, despite ridership beyond initial projections, these places will be all dressed up with nowhere to go. If train service is cancelled, riders will be forced back onto I-35 or the airlines, either less environmentally friendly or convenient, and the region will have lost an important resource. And the passengers a unique experience.

RUNNING ON EMPTY
A Meditation

Road map in my hand, my eyes upon the road,
A lot of miles behind me but a long, long way to go.

Fragment of a song heard on an
unidentified c&w station

On the drive northwest from Fort Worth, Texas, to Amarillo on U.S. Highway 287, the landscape of the plains isn't inspiring even if you aren't driving into the teeth of what Texans call a blue norther. That's what I was doing the first Sunday in March, headed toward Phoenix in the aftermath of a storm that had left a blanket of snow on the fields and a treacherous layer of slush on the road. There was a reason for the trip, but while I've never quite agreed that the journey matters more than the arrival, I've increasingly been able to separate them and to submerge myself in trips that clear or at least empty, for a while, my mind of the things which usually occupy it.

Of course, the mind has to find something to work on, even on the Texas plains. Fortunately, even that unpromising territory has enough signs, including billboards and other verbal clues, to provide material: the ironies, or not, in "Hopewell Cemetery"; the chutzpah in "We buy junk and sell antiques"; the post-lipstick feminism in Armstrong County's "Carmella Jones, Sheriff." "Tornado Museum." Childress, Texas, where signs bearing family names and local references peel above empty buildings next to gleaming plastic signs of franchise restaurants and chain stores. Memphis, where the locals have collapsed and the franchises haven't arrived.

Other signs: the first tumbleweed. The humps—not high

enough to be called hills, not broad enough to be called mesas—that hint that the plains are ending, though the mountains of New Mexico are still hours away even at seventy miles per hour on a highway that, despite its divided four lanes, has the feel of an empty country road.

But at the apex of the angle with Interstate 40, which I joined east of Amarillo and would follow all the way to Flagstaff, Arizona, long lines of semitrailer trucks head in each direction. That Sunday the lines were even longer than usual. Perhaps the drivers had to make deliveries on Monday. Perhaps they had been delayed by the snow across the Texas Panhandle. At one exit ramp leading to a truck stop, the semis were backed up in a double line almost to the highway. Farther west, I was sandwiched between two large trucks, perhaps fifteen feet ahead of and behind my bumpers. Twice the traffic slowed well below the seventy-mile-an-hour speed limit and then came to a stop. The first halt was apparently caused by drivers slowing to look at a trailer overturned in the median. The second came at the inspection station at the New Mexico border where trucks blocked one lane of the interstate.

Because of the traffic, there wasn't much time to look at scenery, but there wasn't much to miss after the so-called Cadillac Ranch—a row of cars sunk into the earth at the same angle by an eccentric local millionaire—and the huge and smelly feed lot for cattle at the pathetically named village of Wildorado. Fortunately, the public radio station in Amarillo plays jazz, and that carried me to the point in New Mexico where mesas and then mountains begin to vary the landscape and further slow traffic as the trucks labor up the increasingly steep grade that culminates in the Sandia Mountains just east of Albuquerque.

Eastern New Mexico doesn't offer much more to look at than the Texas Panhandle. It doesn't have as strong a Hispanic heritage as the rest of the state, partly because the fierce Comanche Indians made it inaccessible to Spanish incursion from the south. But like the rest of the United States, and even more obviously because of the lack of external stimulus, it was already multicultural before liberals and conservatives began to debate about recognizing various heritages. The battle was over before it started. There's jazz, an African American form, on one radio station; Irish and Irish-American music (St. Patrick's Day is near) on another. A Stuckey's convenience store, the only building or indeed human artifact in sight (one of a long chain whose first link lies in the American South and is most famous for its deathly sweet pecan log rolls) has a sign offering cappuccino to the traveler. Another Stuckey's offers "authentic Kachina figures," though it is doubtful that they were fashioned by the Hopi, several hundred miles to the west.

The motto on every New Mexico license plate reads "Land of Enchantment." That becomes true only at Albuquerque, which slopes several thousand feet from the Sandia Mountains to the Rio Grande. From the interstate, the extinct volcanoes on the West Mesa are highlighted against the horizon, and during the long climb up the slope away from the river toward the continental divide, with glimpses of unexpected mountains far north and south, the steep reddish sides of the mesas glow in the morning sun and bound the highway and the railroad through the lava fields at Grants, past Thoreau (named not for the writer but for a railroad official) to Gallup and the Arizona border.

Then, in the long run to Flagstaff, the emptiness as you run through the edge of the Navajo Reservation, accompanied by its radio station broadcasting partly in English, partly in Navajo (sprinkled with untranslatable English phrases like "be on time"), with occasional tribal chants between so-called country and western music and sales pitches for automobiles and other necessities of modern desert life. Multiculturalism again; an ancient language and culture communicated electronically.

Then, from eighty miles away, the first sight of Humphrey's Peak, highest point in Arizona. Flagstaff at its foot and the first real trees in hundreds of miles, south on Interstate 17 and signs reading "Watch for animals next 60 miles," the first time such a warning has been necessary. Then off the Mogollon Rim to the Verde River, the cliffs of Sedona visible to the west; over another mountain range; down the long slope past stands of saguaro cactus, branches like arms angled upward from the elbow; into metropolitan Phoenix, sprawled along the bed of Gila River, sucked dry before it reaches the city.

I had come for several reasons, all having to do with the intersection of family and business concerns. The business got done and the family interacted with. All very pleasant, but I made no connection between my stay and the trip out, nor did I look ahead to the trip back. People mattered; not the place. In fact, Phoenix offers a great deal to assault the senses but not much to stimulate the imagination. Any given neighborhood or suburb looks pretty much like any other. With its six-lane streets and fast-moving traffic, it feels a lot like Lubbock, Texas, with the addition of palm and orange trees and some humpbacked mountains jutting unaccountably out of the landscape.

But being there must do something to the mind, because the trip back has a very different feel. That's partly because there's less sense of anticipation than on the way out. But there's also a stronger sense of gradation and nuance because there's less for the eye to look at and the mind to ponder.

Or less man-made material. Past Table Mesa Road, a bilingual redundancy, and the various signs warning motorists not to pick up hitchhikers who may be escaped prisoners, there is the long climb up the escarpment toward Cordes Junction. The saguaro cactus thins out until, at an unmarked elevation, it gives way to short grass, then to pine forests, and, just east of Flagstaff, to desert again.

Moving east, one has the sense that everything natural is, in the philosophical sense, *necessary*. That is, there is a sufficient reason for everything. Elevation and rainfall account for everything that grows out of the ground; hydrology, geology, vulcanology for everything it grows from. Or doesn't, as in the earth near Holbrook soaked by a rare rainstorm (it follows me for two days) that looks both moist and sterile.

In the midst of this necessity, humans and their constructs seem more and more contingent, so that the power plant at Joseph City seems more startling and intrusive when approached from the west. Although the materials of the infrastructure are naked to the eye, they lack sufficient reason. It's true that the railroad and the highway, always within sight of each other, seek the easiest and most direct routes, but the rivers and washes (rarely wet, incipient canyons in geologic time) move inexorably, uninfluenced by politics or other considerations not visible to the naked eye.

In eastern terms, the desert looks so empty that anything begins to seem possible. And the mind seeks to fill the space. This may explain why ascetics, mystics, and visionaries of all sorts have been attracted to the desert. Sometimes they see only a mirage, like the delusive sight of water down the road; sometimes an equally chimerical cosmic nexus, like the Harmonic Convergence points at Sedona and other suddenly fashionable points in the New Age landscape. Alien presence seems possible when the observer is self-perceived as alien.

And of course land is cheap—a few dollars per month per acre east of Holbrook—because it seems undesirable. But wherever a half-dozen gather together, a developer is in their midst. The true seekers are surrounded by acolytes seeking—a little less enthusiastically—to escape materialism. And then still less, until Santa Fe becomes an extension of Rodeo Drive in Beverly Hills and the natives cannot afford to live there. Then the true seekers, or nearly true seekers, go elsewhere—Taos and Las Vegas in New Mexico, smaller and smaller mountain towns in Colorado—until they in turn are Guccied beyond recognition.

The mind fills the emptiness with speculation . . . and back into New Mexico, Land of Souvenirs as well as Enchantment. Gallup, for some reason less visible than on the westward trip. The Giant truck stop, with its own oil refinery, in the middle of nowhere. Between the mirrored halves of strip development on opposite sides of the interstate in Continental Divide. Souvenirs, but no gas pumps or places to sleep because Whiting Bros. has closed, here and all over the Southwest and even the Stuckey's has failed, which shows that God is just if not consistent.

East of Albuquerque, the mind turns again to man-made objects. Cline's Corners, ancestor of Giant truck stops and other isolated roadside refuges for motorists dotted across the west. Like Giant to the west and Flying C to the east, unlike the authentically deserted fake ghost town and the several failed Stuckey's along the way, it's on the north side of the road. Why? Lord knows there's plenty of land on both sides, and Cline's Corners has moved several times to stay with the shifting route of Highway 66 and later Interstate 40. Perhaps because westward travelers, shocked by the distance between the smallest towns, were more likely than those eastbound and inured to the vastness, to pull in for gas, drinks, a restroom—but never a place to sleep.

(True, Twin Arrows and Jackrabbit in Arizona may or may not cling to survival on the south side of the interstate. But the Navajo Reservation lies to the north, and in any case, they were on the north side of Route 66.)

By the time I've worked this out, I'm past Santa Rosa and the Pecos River and Tucumcari and the high mesa the Comanches used as watchtower and landmark—the last or first natural feature of any note in eastern New Mexico. And to the Texas border, end of Mountain Time and beginning of Central Time. Out of the west of imagination to where speculation seems impossible. Now five hours and three hundred dull and duller miles, measured by clock and odometer, toward home.

PANHANDLING

The "Hard Amarillo Highway" is U.S. 87 north and south, but the drive east and west on Interstate 40 is hard in a different way from that of the redneck rebel native of the Texas Panhandle that Terry Allen sings about. The sign at the state line reads, "Drive Friendly, the Texas Way," and to the long-distance traveler that means clench your teeth and sphincter and drive real fast.

That's because Texas does not, like its Oklahoma and New Mexico neighbors, greet visitors with information or, more important, a rest stop until well into the Panhandle, and, from the west, not until Amarillo. The lack of information is understandable—coming east, there is nothing in the Panhandle to tempt the traveler to veer off north or south, and not much dead ahead, and very little coming west. But the same could be said for Oklahoma, and, except for the grave of Billy the Kid, New Mexico, which has towns or at least geographic sites like House and Field.

Coming west to the Panhandle gives the traveler a certain sense of exhilaration just because it is Texas and not Oklahoma. Furthermore, the eastern side has the only topographic features in the Panhandle visible from I-40 and what remains of Route 66: the red slopes and canyons of the Caprock that provide vistas of dramatic empty space to the north. Near the New Mexico line, there are a few humps not big enough to be called mesas and a conical hill with what looks like a cork. But that's humorous rather than picturesque.

But coming east, Texas is in Central, not Mountain, Time, and it's not New Mexico, much more varied and exotic in people and landscape, and much friendlier in terms of places to pee. Besides, east is the way home, and there's less sense of anticipation.

The first town you get to is Vega—not even, like its counterparts in Nevada and New Mexico, plural. The Texas version bills itself as "Crossroads of the Nation," but even the Moldovan Chamber of Commerce, if there is one, might shrink from having this spot mark the X.

Mostly the Panhandle landscape is so flat and unrelieved that the locals have to construct vertical objects to relieve the monotony. Stanley Marsh 3's Cadillac Ranch just west of Amarillo between exits 60 and 62 (see roadsideamerica.com for history and photos) features ten Cadillacs, 1949 to 1963 vintages, buried grille-first "at the same angle as the Cheops' pyramids." Every time I've driven past, at least in daylight, at least one car has stopped in homage or wonder or just plain puzzlement.

No one has to stop to get a good look at the largest cross in the Western Hemisphere at Groom since it can be seen for at least ten miles in either direction, but there is a little more to see there: stations of the cross, and maybe even a restroom, in which case the church is more charitable than the state. And it's lit for night viewing. Once it had a Christian balloon festival, featuring one shaped like Jesus. (If you don't believe me, check merritministry.org.)

In Groom, at any rate, God has out-topped Mammon. Just east of Groom proper, the leaning (water) tower of Britton tilts eastward, the landmark for what was once a large truck stop whose pumps and buildings have disappeared over the years until only a diesel repair shop stands. It may or may not be open, though one of the large doors is.

Otherwise, nothing much sticks out of the ground except mesquite and the occasional grain elevator, though even those are rare, and there aren't many landmarks to go by unless you've been through the Panhandle many times and create your own. One exception is the recurrent sign for the Big Texan, offering a 72-ounce steak free if the diner can finish it in an hour. And the restaurant itself is painted garish yellow. Just east of that sight, near the Amarillo airport, a former railroad right-of-way is now used to display used machines of various kinds and in various states of disrepair, including, as backdrop, some paraplegic Boeing 727s.

To the eastern eye, the Panhandle is unrelieved. There may be some curves in the highway, but I can't think of many except for lane shifts made necessary by road repair. The mind has to operate on whatever it can find. And create its own surprises, find its own ironies, make up stories. How many vegans live in Vega? What would they eat? That's if they are plural. How would their neighbors regard them? What happened to the Landers of Landergin? (In fact, the founders' name was Landergin, but the traveler has no immediate access to that information.) The grain elevator, gas station, and café are deserted.

Wildorado sounds promising, as if Randolph Scott might be pacing down the middle of the main street toward Barton MacLane. In fact, most of the gas stations and cafés are closed, and the only reason to remember the town—a good one—is the huge feed lot to the east, where fattening cattle stand on hills of their predecessors' dung and the traveler has to hold the nose as well a clench other portions of the anatomy.

The radio does begin to work again. Coming from the west, after miles of watching the auto-search run up and down the dial, stopping only for static on the AM setting, one can finally get clear reception. On AM, sports and talk radio that make Dr. Laura seem like a major intellectual force. On FM, the usual formats, with one surprise: a twenty-four-hour all-blues station in Amarillo that carries maybe a twenty-five-mile radius and, astonishingly, seems to have plenty of advertisers.

And there are other drivers to watch and speculate about, since most present no problems. On two-lane highways, other cars are potential obstacles to progress or threats to safety. The guy in the red pickup with roll bars who passes you at ninety miles an hour on a yellow line is not only a hazard but a stupid bleeping bleep. On the interstate, one can regard him philosophically, even indulgently, since he will occupy any state patrol officer for the next ten miles or so.

Terry Allen's songs seem especially bleak because his characters drive at night and never encounter another car. Things aren't that bad by day in real life, but in the Panhandle, any human presence seems welcome, so that other cars and their drivers become almost companionable sights, like the Rav-4 with Georgia plates I ran with on my last trip east. As you and they vary speeds, you can see the occupants from both sides, drinking coffee, consulting maps, sleeping, sometimes, but not often, glancing at you. If the vehicle is striking enough, you may realize that you play a kind of leap-frog with it as one and then the other stops for gas or a meal and almost regret it when they exit because that's one less thing to think about on the Panhandle.

DOWN HOME

FAMOUS FOR FIFTEEN MINUTES

Since 1958, I've spent more time in Hungary than I have in Missouri. Most of those years I tried to act like an English professor with a proper background. That did not include Boonville.

But the Danube made me think about the Missouri River, and after a number of false starts, I wrote *Mid-Lands: A Family Album*. There is a good deal about my family in the book, but it is really about Boonville, and by extension a large part of middle America, as it looked to a growing boy between the end of World War II and the Eisenhower presidency.

I sent the manuscript to a friend who had published a similar book, and his main concern was how the people I mentioned were going to react. He had found that people would flatly deny saying things that he had taped.

That wasn't a problem with my immediate family, I thought, because I had been sending them chapters as I finished them. They were happy to accept what I did say because they knew what I could have said and didn't. Besides, my family likes outrageous stories.

In fact, the book became a family project. My sister asked her husband to take some photos of the family home and my brother tracked down shots of the church and school we had gone to. Both of them started a word-of-mouth sales campaign and kept asking me when it would be out.

As the publication date approached, they began to have minor doubts. My brother is a county commissioner, and he realized that not everybody might think I was as funny as he did. Even my sister had a brief twinge of prudence. "I hope people like this book," she said, "because there's a picture of my house in it." And she complained that the only photo of her in the book identifies the dog by name, but not her. (That's Beth Davis McClary holding the chicken.) But both of them were enthusiastic about my coming home to promote the book.

The first readers didn't have any stake in the book, but they said very nice things about it in their reviews. The Boonville radio station had me on for a phone interview right after the announcement of the menu at the Senior Citizen's Center—chicken fried steak. A journalism student from MU's KBIA did a phone interview and said that he enjoyed it. He wanted to talk about the divisions that run through the book—blacks and whites, grownups and kids, and so on.

He was especially interested in the divisions between me and my parents. Actually, I told him, I was a lot less concerned with those, having raised a family myself, than I would have been at his age. The conflicts were less important than what I had got from them. After I hung up the phone, I realized that I felt the same way about Boonville.

When I drove up from Oklahoma, I stopped in Kansas City to tape a TV spot for public television with John Masterman. John is a few years older than I and a Yankee—he grew up in Ithaca, New York—but he recognized the picture I had drawn.

When I said that I was on my way to Boonville, he asked, "Don't you find every corner haunted?" Never occurred to me, I said. I remember the past, and I have come to value it more than I expected to, but I don't live in it. A lot of people don't know I'm alive. When the local paper carried a story about the book, they had to identify me as "brother of John Davis, Cooper County commissioner."

But when I got to Boonville, a lot of the past turned up at the old jail, now headquarters of the Friends of Historic Boonville. People kept saying, "I bet you don't recognize me." Hell, I wouldn't recognize *me* if I hadn't been here all this time.

One person I didn't recognize had been a pretty, rather fragile-seeming girl two classes behind me who had married the best-looking boy in my class. She didn't seem fragile anymore—the bone structure held up; she works for a stockbroker and does radio spots. She was very funny about trying to lose her mid-Missouri accent. I was gratified to learn that her husband had lost more of his hair than I had.

A young woman I had never seen asked me to sign the book to someone named Haller. Any relation to Eddie Haller? Her father, she said, and was astonished when I showed her his name in the book.

She was glad that someone had the ability to write all this down. I was pleased every time someone said this, and in different ways they said it fairly often. A high school friend's mother called to say so. A childhood friend called to complain that his wife had bought him a copy and wouldn't give it to him because she was reading it herself. I could hear her laughing in the background, the best kind of review.

Next morning I joined my brother for the early morning coffee bunch at Stephanie's in downtown Boonville. That is a tougher audience. Bill Barlow came home after a career in the Air Force to run an insurance agency and to be unofficial historian of the now-defunct Catholic high school. He pointed out that the picture of the school was backward. He filled in a couple of details I had speculated about. But he liked the fact that I didn't sound like a professor: "When you *mean* 'shit,' you *say* 'shit.'"

It was nice to be in a place where that didn't get me into trouble. In fact, I realized later, a lot of what I had thought of as my unique style was in fact local idiom I had learned before I could read.

Bob Dyer was there too. We had in common the only (graying) beards in the restaurant and the fact that we have both published books about Boonville. His is factual and straightforward; mine is not. So there was no professional rivalry. He gave me a lot of information about the region—he's collecting folktales—and said that someone had written on the men's room wall, "Boonville, where are your poets?" Then he pointed to me and himself for an answer.

"Well," I said, "you wouldn't want to hold your breath until you could think of a third."

After these official and unofficial appearances, I was free to wander around. People would look closely at me and say, "Aren't you John Davis's brother?" or "Aren't you the author?"

But mostly I just hung out. What does the prodigal son do in Boonville? The first thing I do is switch the car radio to AM to listen to the very local radio. (At night they play Billie Holiday and other jazz figures; that's new.)

I notice things that are gone: the Missouri Farmer's Association building where I worked in 1952; the trees and brush in most of the valleys that wind through Boonville; the church I attended.

I eat. Ordinarily, I don't eat gravy from one year to the next. But on my last day in town I had gravy twice, white on biscuits at Stephanie's; brown on hot roast beef at the Stein House for lunch.

I stop by to see people who remember me. They seem to get fewer every year. But some of my contemporaries are coming back to Boonville to retire, so that compensates.

I hang out with family. People are surprised that my brother and sister and I seem to get along pretty well—which we do, as long as we don't push it. Their children are pleasant enough to me as they streak through in pursuit of their own lives.

The young man from KBIA wondered what my attraction to Boonville was. That's simple, I told him: family. But after the visit, this answer seems too simple.

In talking about the book, my brother had used the term "we." That had pleased me more than I could tell him. But the other people in Boonville had responded in the same way, if not the same words.

In writing the book, I came to realize that Boonville was a part of me. In going back, people made me feel that I was a part of Boonville.

BREAKFAST
The Real American Cuisine

Visitors to other countries find it difficult to experience or even to see the ordinary lives of the inhabitants. They go with a battery of stereotypes and clichés, and because these generalizations have considerable surface truth, it is hard to see past them. Of course, the caricatures can give way to more realistic views.

For example, we all have stereotypes about eating habits foreign to us, but if pressed, Americans might concede that Europeans do not always eat at sidewalk cafés, just as Europeans might be able to imagine that Americans could possibly eat somewhere besides fast-food restaurants uniform in appearance and in the taste of the food.

No one should miss the chance to visit symptoms of a culture important enough to become clichés, but there are other ways of observing native life. Visitors to the United States can see ordinary Americans at their best by going out to breakfast on a regular basis and to a particular type of restaurant.

Americans have a mystique about breakfast that probably derives from our past as an agricultural nation. My grandmother's generation sat down to enormous meals—bacon, ham, or sausage (in the Southwest, steak); some variety of fried potatoes; eggs, usually fried or scrambled; bread or biscuits; hot cakes or waffles; in the South, grits (boiled ground corn that sticks between the teeth and to which taste has to be imparted with seasonings); perhaps a hot cereal, usually oatmeal. For a long morning's work in the fields, "eating like a field hand" was necessary. A "continental breakfast," on the other hand, connoted something light, insubstantial, almost effete.

As Americans moved to cities and became more sedentary, the huge breakfast became obsolete, and nutritionists now scold us about the importance of eating at least something nourishing before going to work. However, a number of factors conspire against inherited and scientific wisdom: Americans are most hurried early in the day; children are bombarded with television commercials for various sugared and flavored cold cereals, which may be no less nutritious than oatmeal but do not have its moral authority; eggs contain cholesterol; hotcakes and waffles contain carbohydrates, banned by many diets, and require syrup and butter, banned by every diet, and in any case take time and trouble to prepare.

As a result, many Americans skip breakfast altogether or grab doughnuts or other pastries on the way to work or behave stereotypically and drink "instant breakfast" (powdered material stirred into milk). Some fast-food chains that used to open at lunchtime now serve breakfasts, which my grandmother would have considered shrunken parodies of the meals she fixed.

However, there are still places to get breakfast that is not prepackaged, but to see real Americans, one has to choose carefully. These restaurants are not owned by chains, except the ones with "pancake" or "waffle" in their titles, and they are often named after the proprietor. Sometimes they are called "cafés," like the Main Street Café in my home town. Preferably they should cater, though not exclusively, to working people, or to people going to work. Any place that serves "brunch" (between breakfast and lunch in both time and menu) or even mentions Eggs Benedict on its menu may have much better food and a very civilized atmosphere (i.e., quiet, restrained, elegant, a bit stiff), but it will not be what Ernest Hemingway called, in a very different context and time of day, a clean, well-lighted place.

Absolutely essential, and almost uniformly absent in fancier restaurants, are booths. These give patrons the space, sense of privacy, and leisure required for a pleasant breakfast. Most of these places also have counters, which can be good or bad. One chain restaurant seats all solitary patrons at the counter to make more efficient use of booth space, and because one must face the wall or a serving bar, with the staff scurrying back and forth, this is only satisfactory if all you want to do is eat and leave. Managing a newspaper (an essential part of an ideal breakfast) is almost impossible, for either it has to be folded into quarters, which inhibits leisured glances over the headlines and dilettantish selection of something amusing to read, or the outside edge may dip into a neighbor's maple syrup or congealing egg yolk. This improves neither the newspaper, the food, nor the temper.

The only good thing to be said for tables is that large groups—athletic teams, students on field trips, meetings formal and informal—can be isolated from those with nothing but breakfasting on their minds.

Booths, the more labyrinthine in arrangement the better, are essential because they give a sense of separate space without, unless the backs are very high, cutting off views of other patrons.

The emotional as well as the physical atmosphere should be serious but not formal, open but not too familiar. The staff, mostly women, tends to be more friendly and to enter into conversations more naturally and freely than in more exclusive establishments—and this is true even in supposedly cold and impersonal Manhattan. Service should not be obsequious or unobtrusive—a good sign is someone circulating with a coffee pot to refill cups—but it should not be insistent, and you should not be addressed, as you will in many chain restaurants that do not serve breakfast, as "guys" by the university-aged staff.

Also essential is a cashier's desk. If the waiter or waitress brings the check on a tray, this is the wrong kind of restaurant. The cashier's desk provides a physical transition to the outside world; the open exchange of money for service symbolizes the unabashed connection to the economic realities patrons go forth to face.

My affection for the right kind of café is obviously more social than gustatory. I associate eating breakfast in a restaurant either with going somewhere and doing something new and significant or, in later years, with relaxed self-indulgence. My grandmother's breakfasts were for people who worked hard, and perhaps this affected one of my happiest memories from boyhood, having rolls and coffee all by myself, just before daybreak, a hundred miles from home in a real city, while my father bought supplies at the fruit and vegetable market. Everyone was working or getting ready to work, but no one hurried, and though the sense of freedom, independence, and adulthood may have been illusory, the illusion was important to a boy of ten. Perhaps as a result, I have never felt alien in any city.

More than half a century later, my children almost the age my father was then, I look at the other patrons less wide-eyed, but with no less enjoyment. The children—and American children or for that matter their parents are not at their best in restaurants—seem to share my sense that this is an unusual and important occasion and tend to behave far more maturely than their years. They are rested, freshly scrubbed and dressed, and alert without being overexcited. It is even possible to delude oneself into believing in the original innocence fancifully described by Romantic poets.

Fulfilled rather than expectant are the couples, especially on weekends, more especially on Saturdays, when they are not mixed with the churchgoing crowds. Married or not, if they like each other well enough to share breakfast, romance is not dead. Age and class do not matter. I prefer mature couples casually dressed. These couples do not hurry; they are neither indifferent to nor obsessed with each other; they give the impression of being satisfied but not satiated. They may share a newspaper and pay only casual attention to each other, and they are enough at ease not to worry about appearances. They are one of the best expressions I know of heterosexual pairing.

During the week, the patrons are mostly working people, in the Southwest, mostly working men. They give a focus and a point to the restaurant, for it is their activity that makes the leisure of other patrons meaningful.

In the Great Plains, the working men come from a few select groups—artisans, repairmen, farmers, ranchers—who do not have formally established working hours. Their presence can be detected even in the parking lot because of their pickup trucks, sometimes muddy and battered and often filled with exotic tools. Inside, the owners are easily recognizable: they sit sideways in the booths, wearing billed caps that bear patches advertising portable or self-propelled agricultural or industrial machinery. (Patches advertising beer or other consumer goods indicate a lack of seriousness.) In the

Southwest, caps are replaced by cowboy hats. Burned by wind and sun, these men are literally rednecks (a term used to designate white Southern men of rural background and blue-collar habits and occupation). They carry on banter among themselves and with the waitresses in stylized and jocular fashion, and they form a closed but not hostile group that the outsider is free to observe but not invited to join. They create the atmosphere of an informal private club, which makes the restaurant a pleasure to visit.

(I've described a male atmosphere. A woman friend reminded me that for women, breakfast is not preparation for work; it *is* work. A veteran of twenty-five years of marriage and three children, she observed that the only time a woman feels guiltless about eating a breakfast that she hasn't cooked is when she is traveling, when she is given breakfast on Mother's Day, and when her house has burned down.)

After 10 A.M. or so, when the workers have stretched coffee breaks as far as they can, the atmosphere changes. Workers let loose for lunch create a sense of urgency; mere idlers provide what business there is during the afternoon. And really, there is no reason to eat in this kind of restaurant except at breakfast. You can get lunch or dinner, but the atmosphere will not compensate for the plain quality of the food because "home cooked" often means that the vegetables have been boiled almost to disintegration, there will be grease circles in the gravy pooled in undistinguished mashed potatoes, and the salad will be limp and unimaginative.

Breakfast is harder, though not impossible, to ruin, and in any case, the company and the atmosphere will show the visitor unique and valuable aspects of American life.

CONSULT YOUR LOCAL LISTING

Those who spend a lot of time driving the interstates don't have to be told that radio in America is becoming more and more homogenized, largely because fewer and fewer companies own more and more stations. And with the new technology of satellites and digital programming, owners find it cheaper to pipe in programming than to hire even the cheapest help to broadcast live.

One notable, and noble, exception, known to everybody who hits the search button on the AM band between Grants, New Mexico, and Flagstaff, Arizona, is KTNN, "The Navajo Nation," broadcasting from Window Rock, Arizona, which sounds like nothing you've heard anywhere else. You might recognize the voice of Lee Ann Rimes or, if you're old enough, Webb Pierce, but when the cut ends you'll hear, about half the time, an announcement or a commercial in which the singer and tune are the only identifiable words. The rest, rhythmic, with a lot of hesitation between double vowels, is not unpleasing but totally unintelligible. That's because it's Navajo, used in World War II by Navajo radio operators, or code-talkers, to transmit information in a way that the Japanese, or for that matter most of the world, never could break.

Furthermore, you will hear the station for a long time, because it has a 50,000-watt clear-channel license, the last one granted by the FCC. In 1982, the commercial license was put up for bid, and in 1984 the FCC, then pro-minority business, granted it to the Navajo

Nation on the grounds that the widely flung population, in an area larger than West Virginia and a whole lot less densely populated, had no common means of communication. They do since 1986, when the station opened. Later the Nation got a license for KWRK-FM, but the signal has a radius of 100 miles and is directed to a younger, English-speaking audience. During the day, KTNN's signal reaches almost 33,000 square miles in the Four Corners area (New Mexico, Arizona, Utah, and Colorado), most of that the Navajo Reservation. That puts it eighth in area of coverage behind stations in some very flat states. At night, it reaches well into the Pacific Ocean and up as far as Washington.

There are other stations owned and run by Native Americans (most people in Indian country, including Native Americans, say "Indians"). Two of them, WASG, owned by the Creek in Alabama, and WYRU, owned by the Lumbee in North Carolina, are also commercial. Twenty-seven other native-owned stations, many in Alaska, are affiliated with public radio, including stations of much smaller wattage run by the Navajo, Zuni, Jicarilla Apache, and other tribes in the New Mexico–Arizona area. Some commercial stations in Farmington and Gallup run commercials, but no programming, in Navajo.

But these other native-owned stations cover very small areas and feed in a good deal of their programming from National Public Radio. KTNN does original programming for much of the day. From 5 A.M. to 2 P.M., it plays twelve songs an hour: four native songs, one native-contemporary, three "recurrent," two top 40, an oldie, and one "KT music," which may explain the song I heard that sounded like Native American reggae. Most of the music is standard country and western, with a heavy emphasis on tunes and artists I haven't heard since the 1950s, because, general manager Tazbah McCullah says, the lifestyle dictated that choice.

The music is interspersed with news and weather, in English and Navajo, rodeo and sports coverage, announcements of funerals (introduced by "Jesus Is Calling") and other communal and tribal events, and public service programming. Commercials, in English or Navajo, cover the usual range—car and truck dealers, restaurants, goods and services, "Alter-Native" concerts. Most advertisers seem to be local, at least by the relaxed standards of open country, and many are from Flagstaff, about 180 miles from Window Rock.

After 2 P.M., much of the programming is in English, but there's a call-in show, with a set topic—consolidating youth programs on the day I passed through—that sometimes becomes acrimonious, especially around tribal election time.

Evening hours are devoted to native music, other specialty programs, and sports—Phoenix Suns, Arizona Cardinals, Northern Arizona University. Some of the broadcasts are in Navajo—the Suns by a Navajo sand-painter, the Cardinals by the only woman NFL broadcaster. The sports programming helps to sell the airtime.

From midnight to 5 A.M., KTNN is turned over to the Interstate Radio Network, which targets over-the-road truck drivers. The only revenue from this programming is from commercials on the feed. KTNN's sales staff doesn't try to go beyond the local market.

Even for the target audience, commercials can be a problem. KTNN, like other stations, can't advertise tobacco, and because of obvious problems on the reservation, they won't advertise alcohol. And the management is not always happy about ads that are borderline deceptive. However, enough advertisers want to target the 200,000 Navajos in the listening area to keep the station solvent.

Of course, there is competition, and, says McCullah, there will be more and more from satellite, which will allow listeners to choose highly specialized programming and fragment the audience for KTNN and every other commercial station, much like the effect of cable on network and local television.

But KTNN has problems that other stations don't. Recruiting staff presents special problems. Announcers have to be fluent in spoken English and Navajo, and they have to read English well enough to be able to translate readily into Navajo. Social problems on the reservation don't pass by the KTNN staff, and there is considerable turnover. However, KTNN pays better than other stations in the market, and in any case its competitors prefer professionally trained people, so that people in the better jobs tend to stay.

Another problem comes from the fact that the station has gone digital, and many otherwise qualified people have trouble with the technology, so the management has to keep doing in-service training. And digital causes other difficulties. Listeners have trouble with the idea that the person they're hearing isn't actually in the studio, and visits from school groups have dropped off because the kids can't say, "Hi, Mom" in real time. And once, on a remote, the computer went out and the announcers had to go live. Some of the younger ones didn't know what to do with the CDs.

Another problem, linguistic rather than technical, is that an announcement in Navajo takes about a minute longer than the English version, and that affects timing. For example, in a Navajo-English dictionary of health-related terms, three or four lines are needed to render "self-expression" in Navajo. Football is *jool ne ite l igii*; the Arizona Cardinals are *Taa ya nii t oshi*, or "the bird with the feather on its head"; a huddle is *Ninaanijee do yiniye ninaada-hat a.*

As a bilingual station, KTNN gets complaints in and about both languages. Some listeners complain that there is too much English, either in straight programming or interspersed in Navajo announcements, as in "be on time" or in times and scores of rodeo winners. Others contend that Navajo words are mispronounced, perhaps because eastern and western Navajo dialects differ slightly. Still others complain about coinages or compressions—to move things along—but one bilingual teacher, in an interview on KTNN, defended innovations on the grounds that Navajo, like other languages, has to keep changing and growing to deal with new experience. When the Navajo first got wagons, he says, they had to be able to name the parts. The same thing is true of more recent technology, like computers.

Language is crucial to KTNN's mission, McCullah says. Without programming in Navajo, the station will be just another money-maker. Despite an attempt to foster the language in Head Start programs, many children don't know Navajo because many of their teachers don't. The younger generation—more than half the population—will have to keep the language alive in order for KTNN to fulfill its cultural mission.

And, incidentally, give the transient audience along Interstate 40 and the north-south highways a sense of life in the Navajo Nation and a chance to hear music that no other station would play, like the traditional chant—drums, deep male voices in unison—whose words sound almost familiar and turn out to sing the praises of Looney Tunes cartoons, because everyone likes to laugh.

REINVENTIONS

BLACKWATER COMES BACK

To the casual visitor, Blackwater, Missouri, looks a lot like hundreds of other farm towns in the Midwest. The frame houses and yards may be a little neater than in most such towns, and the one-block, mostly brick business district has most of the buildings occupied and signs of work on those that aren't, and there are new brick sidewalks, a garden, and new, working, period street lamps.

The most unusual thing about Blackwater is that it exists at all. Less than ten years ago, the mayor of the town predicted that it would soon disincorporate, not long after the centenary of its founding in 1887.

Into the 1940s, when it was incorporated with a population of 650, the town prospered in a modest way. Established as a water stop when the Missouri Pacific Railroad was completed, the railway hotel, grain elevator, and other farm-related businesses formed the heart of the town. But roads got better; people began to shop and work in Boonville, the county seat fifteen miles away, and business and population dwindled. The high school was abolished in 1945. The Missouri Farmers Association closed its Blackwater operation in the late 1960s.

By 1970, when the Missouri Pacific depot was torn down for the lumber, Estil Oswald, a local farmer, was using most of the buildings in the business district to store a large collection of low-end antiques. The rock quarry east of town had flooded, and the Danner family, who had moved to Blackwater in 1962, had turned it into a swimming and picnic area called Wildcliff.

The 1980s saw further decline. High interest rates hurt the farmers. A flood and increased insurance costs meant the end of Wildcliff, and the Danners moved their center of operations to New Orleans, where they still own a hotel and yacht service. The buildings housing antiques were deteriorating beyond the point of usefulness, and the shops closed. By the early 1990s, only four of the twenty-two business buildings were occupied: a bank, a post office, a farm supply store, and an auto body shop. The whole east side was vacant. Oswald had given three buildings to another local man to get rid of liability. He sold them for $200 to William "Sonny" Green, who planned to demolish them and use the lots for used equipment. Another building was offered to the city, and the city refused to accept it.

Several other buildings collapsed, and a local arsonist and one-man crime wave set fire to two others. (He also painted the railroad warning lights black, uncoupled train cars, and, according to legend, added unspecified body fluids to the special sauce at the nearest Taco Bell. He also sent love letters to local males, one of whom discovered him in his closet, beat him severely, realized that the intruder had appropriated his clothing, and said, "Don't you dare bleed on my shirt!")

Some official help proved no more productive. A grant from the state proved the adage, "With friends like that, who needs enemies?" An experimental sewer system was installed in the mid-1980s, featuring a Rube Goldberg arrangement of grinders and pumps at each house, with an elaborate electrical warning system that set off bells when the system malfunctioned, as it often did, so that the whole town's sewage could back up into one yard or even toilet. No local electrician knew anything about the system, and Mary Watson, a former mayor, remembers having to carry an adjustable wrench in her purse. Her breaking point came one Christmas Eve at 2 A.M., in the middle of a wind-driven snowstorm, when an elderly woman called to report that her bell had gone off.

Blackwater could have become like Nelson, a few miles down the track, whose teenagers used to look down on Blackwater. Now the two-block business district has collapsed, and you can't even buy a

Coke. In another nearby town, a mayoral candidate ran on the platform, "Don't let us be another Blackwater." The town had been deteriorating for years.

Now it was in danger of becoming derelict. Unlike nearby Arrow Rock, first stop on the Santa Fe Trail and now a state historical site and tourist destination deserted on weekdays, it has no real historical significance. It has no ability to attract industry with materials or workforce. The only thing left was nostalgic charm, and it didn't have any.

The catalyst to help give Blackwater some was Bobby Danner, youngest member of the family. He had been traveling widely, one language area at a time (South America and Spain, Italy, France), working at intervals in the family hotel, in a building saved by preservationists. In 1993, at the age of twenty-five, he decided that it was time to do something with his life. He tried to join the Peace Corps, but he did (and does) not have a college degree. On a visit to Blackwater, he remembered Gabriel Garcia Marquez's *One Hundred Years of Solitude,* with its deserted village in the jungle, and he decided to try to save and restore the town.

He ran for mayor—Blackwater is still a fourth-class city because of a grandfather clause—and became the youngest mayor in Missouri. His first job was to convince the city council to pass zoning and property maintenance ordinances, and after a stiff battle, some younger council members pushed these through. The school history club had already been formed and had cleaned up a nearby cemetery. The city got a grant to rehabilitate nineteen houses and demolish another. It was the first of many the city applied for and received, and the Neighborhood Assistance Program, which gives tax credits and is repaid, continues to provide loans for remodeling of old buildings and inventory for new businesses. Voters passed a bond issue and, more remarkably, the city was able to sell the bonds to replace the disastrous sewer experiment. The Blackwater Preservation Society was founded, and recently it has been joined by the Blackwater Community Club, which has advertised the town in print and with a sign at the I-70 exit that brings increasing numbers of visitors.

Community involvement has been crucial. The 1920-vintage concrete sidewalks were in terrible shape. Randy Widel, a local contractor, donated the use of equipment to remove them; the city bought 25,000 bricks; and people in the community learned to lay them. The street lamps were donated by local businesses and families. A garden was planted in a gap left by a building that had collapsed.

Not everyone was pleased. One citizen came to city hall on election day, plunked down his water meter, and announced that he was removing himself from the city water system. (Improving the water, from a plant built in the 1940s, is the next project; the mayor has to back-flush the system every day, which accounts for most of his income as a city official.) Another, upset by the zoning ordinance, took to photographing the mayor "not living in Blackwater," though that seems difficult to demonstrate with still photos.

Bonnie Rapp says that city council meetings last a long time because the members sit around and tell stories, and in Cooper County, stories sometimes seem to be more important than facts. The volunteer fire department's motto is reported to be "We never lost a basement yet," or in another version immediately offered, "We saved the lot." Their greatest success was saving the hotel after coming back from another fire. The tank had been drained, so the truck drew water from the flooded Blackwater River, which had risen near enough for the hoses to reach.

The council isn't besieged by outraged citizens because, Bonnie Rapp says, those turn up at all hours, every day, at city hall to vent their grievances. Bonnie, who has been city clerk since 1984, seems to be able to deal with them and with anyone else who shows up. When the town erected a windmill on the site of the original well, a representative from the highway department objected to the encroachment on state property. Bonnie told him that three months previously, the city had asked his department to fix potholes in the street—and the reply was that the department owned the roadway but not the median. He left and hasn't returned.

After dealing with the infrastructure, Blackwater turned attention to the buildings in the business district. Sonny and Dorothy Green bought an abandoned, roofless restaurant to salvage the kitchen equipment and then decided to fix up the building and, though they had no experience in the restaurant business, to open Green's, which in October, 2000, was for sale, though they are in no hurry. How's business? "We can't complain," Dorothy says, and in

Cooper County that translates into wild enthusiasm. Sonny sold the other three buildings for a 750 percent profit and now admits that Bobby Danner had a better idea.

Harold (Buddy) Gibson, a former resident whose father had been mayor of Blackwater, came back from California and was appalled at the condition of the town. He bought two houses, where he and his wife and sometimes his daughters live in June and October, mid-Missouri's best months, and several buildings in the business district, including what is now the post office and the former Huffman's store, cornerstone on the east side of Main Street.

That was in deplorable condition: the roof leaked (like most of those in that row); the floor was ruined; windows were broken; the catwalks along the interior walls fallen in. He received a Neighborhood Assistance Program loan from the Missouri Department of Economic Development through the Blackwater Preservation society, fixed the roof, and hired some local Amish to put in a rough oak floor. Then he asked Bonnie Rapp, also historian and muralist, to repaint the Holsum Bread sign on the west wall. It now is the site of an antique mall.

The Danners have been restoring the rest of the buildings, piecemeal and as needed, using photographs of the town from 1905 as guides. They work fast and hard. Lila Huebert had looked at the Lamine country store, a few miles uptrack on the other road to Arrow Rock as a site for her antique store, but she was worried about structural and security problems. Bobby showed her a building that had old and damaged tile and no ceiling at all and convinced her to locate in Blackwater. He and his brothers dropped everything else to get the building ready for occupancy in a few weeks, including a new, separate restroom clad in siding from a real outhouse and exposed interior brick. In the main building, Lila has a reconstructed outhouse for sale in what is now Back Roads: The Road to Elegant Clutter, which opened in August, 2001.

The building that now houses Antiques and Interiors by Mary Watson has a more elaborate décor. Mary has worked as an interior designer for many years, and she had the walls painted in a deep raspberry and brought in fireplaces from New Orleans. Mark Danner did the wood work here, as he has done for other restorations.

An earlier and bigger project was a handsome two-story building, left by a bank that failed in the depression, soon to open as the Mid-Missouri Museum of Independent Telephone Pioneers, with vintage equipment on display.

As a result of these and other restorations, Blackwater has received awards from the Missouri Community Betterment Association in four of the last five years, winning first place in 1997 and 2000. The National Center for Small Communities gave the mayor an award. *Midwest Living* gave another award to the town.

Blackwater is expanding, modestly, its commercial base. A rural schoolhouse was moved to town and is now an antique shop. The cage in the historic jail has been recovered after its odyssey through half a dozen owners and made the center of a rustic wooden building (not brick, and not by the railroad tracks, Dorothy Green notes). The West End Theater, just ending its fifth year of plays by returned resident Jay Turley featuring local actors, funnels profits into improvements in the town. A rural church will be moved next to the jail. And the Citizen's Community Bank—the second in a town of just over two hundred—has recently moved into its new building.

The occupancy numbers for the original commercial buildings have been reversed: eighteen of twenty-two commercial buildings are occupied. Of those still vacant, one is almost ready for occupancy, once the Masonite siding is removed; another is the warehouse for reconstruction materials; another, used for storage by the Citizen's Bank and Trust, will be converted into city hall when the post office occupies the current building. The bullet chips on the white glazed brick, made by either a judge or a banker in his cups who lived above the bank across the street, will not be repaired because they have historical or at least anecdotal significance.

The fourth building, a major project and anchor of the new Blackwater, is the hotel. The original wooden hotel burned in 1888 and was replaced by the current brick building, which was partially burned in 1993. It is called the Iron Horse in the hope, as one observer says, that passing trains will be considered part of the ambience. The stained glass figure of a phoenix rising from the flames will be installed over the front door.

The hotel is last because Bobby Danner realized that the town had to have a commercial base before the hotel could be viable. The reconstruction was done with private money, for, as one local expert on historic preservation commented, he is building the hotel not as it was but much better. And the hotel has a new and, for Blackwater, very fancy restaurant.

A half-dozen antique stores and a summer repertory theater are not enough to make even an eleven-room hotel profitable. Occupancy rates will depend at least partly on another Danner project, supervised by Bobby's older brother, "Young Jim": a twenty-seven hole golf course, swimming complex, and conference center on the site of Wildcliff.

This development should keep Blackwater economically sound, and the visitors will be transient enough and far enough out of town not to affect its atmosphere. Fahrendorf Supply, probably the oldest business in Blackwater except for the bank, opened in 1905, and Mary Jane Fahrendorf has worked there since 1965 and owned it since 1976. It stocks everything from batteries to hardware to liquor to snack food and probably a lot else. She says that her business has not increased—most of the new people commute to Columbia or Boonville, but that she is happy to see the town's revival.

One indication of the atmosphere is a poster, made by local school children, taped to her counter. It reads, "The only Mary Jane the 5th graders want is the one at Fahrendorf's Supply." Mary Jane thought they couldn't spell marijuana.

Lila Huebert is a newcomer, and she particularly enjoys the small-town atmosphere, where she can leave the store to talk to her neighbors without locking the door. Jerry Butler, who manages the antique mall, lives in Arrow Rock but thinks of moving to Blackwater, though no residential property is currently available, and the newest houses in the city limits were built in the late 1980s. Antiques and Interiors by Mary Watson moved from Columbia. All five Danner siblings have returned to the area, and two are building houses near Blackwater. Ruth Young, at the post office, says that there are a number of new residents on the route and contrasts the vitality of Blackwater with her home town, Bunceton.

Some of the population increase is the result of single-resident households of elderly people being replaced by families. And this was the news most exciting to Bonnie and ex-mayor Mary Watson, who said, "Babies are being born here again."

MOAB, UTAH
Is There Life after Abbey?

> When I return will it be the same? Will I be the
> same? Will anything ever be quite the same again?
>
> Edward Abbey, *Desert Solitaire*

In the late 1950s Edward Abbey was gathering the impressions that
went into *Desert Solitaire*, and ten years later he characterized Moab,
Utah, as one of the "small, rational, beautiful and durable towns"
established by the Mormons "where we can still see the handsome
homes of hand-carved sandstone blocks, the quiet streets lined with
irrigation ditches and giant cottonwoods, the gardens and irrigated
pastures, the children riding their horses, which remind us on the
downhill side of the twentieth century of what life must have been
like back in the nineteenth. On the gentle side, that is."

Abbey preferred the stony landscape of the Arches National Park
and the surrounding canyons and highlands, and at least from the
evidence of his book, he spent as little time as possible in the town.
He knew, of course, that Moab was the center of a uranium boom,
but he must have paid little attention to the actual life of the town. At
least one native thought things anything but rational, since she had
to go to school at 5 A.M. in order to make way for a second shift later
in the day.

In fact, as Jose Knighton's monograph testifies, Moab has been
the site of several booms and almost as many busts in less than
150 years. Cattle had gone bust off and on since the first ranchers
arrived. The population went from 1,200 in 1950 to 5,000 in 1980,
but when I came through Moab in 1987 uranium mining and

120

other extractive industries had sunk so badly that, according to one report, a quarter of the houses were empty. People had abandoned them to the bank, many of them heading for the gold mines of Colorado. While I didn't know how depressed the economy was, I could see that not much was happening. There were two supposedly upscale restaurants, and I chose Mi Vida, the former home of Charles Steen, the uranium tycoon, because of the view. What I saw was a derelict urinating outside the window. The food was as bad as I've eaten anywhere in North America or Europe. Anyway, the town fit the description Abbey gave it in another, less nostalgic, passage in the book as one of "Those hot, dusty, strange and isolated little towns set so far apart from one another, so far from anywhere, in the middle of silence and emptiness and burning rock."

Still, some of the inhabitants found reasons to stay—roots, pure cussedness, a love of the surrounding landscape, and a style of living that had some resemblance to Abbey's vision of the town as a survival of a gracious era. Some settled in. Jim Stiles, who had followed Abbey as a ranger at the Arches in 1976 and later found that even he could afford to buy a house—for $14,000—that today would probably go in the high 80s. He said that the banker he dealt with suddenly realized that he was going to be part of the community and was startled at the idea. (Probably he would have been even more startled had he know that Stiles would found the *Canyon Country Zephyr,* a bi-monthly tabloid full of ads for various tourist-oriented as well as local businesses and diatribes against irresponsible development, idiotic tourists, and the Sierra Club for being soft on so-called modernization. One local criticized Stiles for taking the government's pay and then bad-mouthing it, but that's in the American tradition. They may pay us, but they can't buy us.)

Moab began to come back in 1985 when Slickrock Trail east of town, designed as a dirt bike trail, was turned over to mountain bikers and Rim Cycles began to offer tours. People in Moab invested in the new industry, and Grand County commissioners spent much of the revenue from the transient room tax to foster tourism.

The growing popularity of the Arches helped. In 1985, 363,000 people visited the park; in 1995, 859,000; in 1999, with over a month to go, more than 856,000. More than 1.5 million people go through Moab every year, partly because U.S. Highway 191 provides part of the most convenient truck route between Seattle and Phoenix, which sounds very unlikely until you look at a map.

With numbers like that, Moab was bound to change, and part of the change was internal, or at least not transient. In 1989, the year Abbey died, Jose Knighton founded the Back of Beyond Bookstore to ensure that his books would be available in Moab, and Stiles founded the *Zephyr*. He now admits that he and his kind of people are partly responsible for the town's yuppification. Twenty years ago, he says, people came to Moab with the understanding that they would have fewer services and cultural opportunities. But Stiles and his cohort added some urban-style amenities to what had been a redneck Mormon town, so that less adventurous people decided that it must be a civilized place and helped to change the town still further.

One major change was in real estate prices. Outsiders, especially from California and Colorado, came for the mountain biking, saw that houses were selling for what seemed to them next to nothing, and bought three or four at a time as speculative investments. A standard line heard in real estate offices in town, Stiles maintains, was "What can I steal today?"

Even as late as 1991, a lot in Castle Valley sold for $7,500, a bargain even then. Today, it is worth $40,000 to $50,000. A lot that went for $14,000 in 1993 more than doubled in price two years later and would now go in the high 40s. A 1,620-square-foot house, with a lot of sweat equity, cost $90,000 in 1993 and is now appraised at double that. That is typical. Anyone looking through local real estate brochures, except displaced Californians, is likely to experience sticker shock, and not just at the new houses built in non-vernacular Santa Fe style fake adobe in the foothills southwest of town. And one announcer on KZMU, the local public radio station, doesn't even want to *say* the word "condo" for fear of conjuring up that particular monster. On the same program, a seasonal service worker complained that very soon, and in some cases even now, people like her could not afford to live in Moab.

This situation is not peculiar to Moab. As Hal K. Rothman shows in *Devil's Bargains: Tourism in the Twentieth-Century American West*, the same thing happened in Santa Fe, Aspen and other Colorado ski resorts, Sun Valley, Jackson Hole, and every place else in the West that depends on upscale tourism. (As someone said, in Aspen the billionaires are driving out the millionaires.) And according to the representatives of the local travel council, seventy-five percent of Moab's economy comes from tourism.

And that means commercial development. In 1987, there seemed to be only a few motels that met even my low standards (funky but not lousy). Beginning in the early nineties, various chains entered the market, and now Moab has thirty-five motels and sixteen bed and breakfasts. And seven bicycle dealers, three mountain climbing shops, and fifteen rafting tour guides. Highway 191, which is also Main Street, is lined with trendy shops: outdoor wear, T-shirts, souvenirs, brew pubs, coffee shops, and the usual things one finds in a tourist town. Flanking the town at each end are a water park and a chairlift to the bluffs above, both despised by those who want to preserve Moab as a center of culture and environmental consciousness. Just inside these eyesores, beyond the two-block boutique district, and off the main street lie the stores and institutions used by the locals: Ford and Chevrolet dealerships, hardware and lumber, auto supplies, groceries, workaday clothing, churches, the library, hospital, medical and legal offices.

Still, to do any real shopping or get medical care from specialists, residents have to drive at least two hours to Grand Junction, Colorado, or farther than that to Cortez, Colorado. Moab doesn't even have a Wal-Mart, though you can get Rolfed.

No one I talked to really wants a Wal-Mart, symbol of corporate greed reaching its tentacles into the heart of virtuous small-town America. If Wal-Mart does come, Moabites agree that it will be built south of Moab, just over the Grand County line in San Juan County, home, in local mythology, to the Great Satan of lust for industrial development, pollution, and corruption of an environment that even Moab's boosters are smart enough to recognize as the town's economic as well as spiritual core. For example, the largest private employer in San Juan County—"When fully operating"—is White Mesa Mill, dependent on trucked-in recycled radioactive materials.

Compared to the towns in San Juan County—Monticello, Blanding, and tiny Bluff—Moab is a center of light and reason—and bigger than all these towns put together. The *Times-Independent* in Moab is the only one of three papers in the two counties, all weeklies, to carry anything but local stories. The *San Juan Record* in Monticello and the *Blue Mountain Panorama* in Blanding are full of stories about young people departing for or returning from Mormon missionary work. The San Juan Theater is closed Sundays; family tickets are $16 on Mondays, a bargain for Mormons.

The most dramatic contrast in attitudes is evident in police reports. A woman in Moab, wandering in the middle of the road, called a policeman a "communist vampire" and was sent home with a warning. In Blanding, a Colorado man jack-knifed his trailer in the main street, but his worst offense, according to the editorial comment, was his comment that Lake Powell should be drained. This, the editor felt, was the equivalent of strangers' invading one's living room and taking over, as if national lands belong, by God and Ronald Reagan, to the locals. And judging from one comment—the county commissioners "can't be in too many lawsuits with the Federal Government at one time"—San Juan County is apparently in continuous battle with the Bureau of Land Management over county incursion into national park and forest lands.

The Grand County commissioners and for that matter the city council were not always environmentally conscious, but people who moved to Moab because of the landscape and outdoor lifestyle have moderated official stances and at the very least have made their issues part of public debate. Out of season, the town is tranquil to comatose except on major holidays like Thanksgiving. Many Main Street businesses close for the winter. Others open at ten. One morning I went into the bookstore and found the clerk asleep on a sofa.

Summers are not tranquil. On the door to the janitor's closet at the large and well-stocked visitors' center is a sign that forbids bathing and doing laundry in the sink and another that lists places where, for a small fee, one can shower. And though the large campground north of town is closed in winter, a number of vans and Microbuses park along the east bank of the Colorado River on the outskirts of town. The tourist season is a boon in economic terms but, for many locals, a burden in personal terms.

However, not all of Moab is tourist territory. Driving around the town, one can see that, like much larger towns, it is divided into three parts, if not more. There is the main drag, full of semis all year and bumper to bumper with tourists in the summer. Upslope to the east are scattered the mid-six-figure houses and condos. To the east of Main Street and along Spanish Valley Road to the south is residential and semirural Moab, with horse properties, a few alfalfa fields, and some indigenous and very funky enterprises like the junkyard that's the VW Microbus equivalent of the elephant's graveyard. The people who came for the hiking, biking, and ambiance are visible—lots of bicycles—but not obtrusive except on KZMU, where volunteers like the assistant manager of a hardware store (from Missouri), a high school social studies teacher (from Ohio), and a baker (from the East by way of the Bay Area) host programs like The Lizard Skinner Show (trailer park and wife-beating music) in a consistently mellow atmosphere all year round. New Age attitudes are present but not yet predominant.

The question is how long Moab can stay mellow. Jim Stiles says that current zoning allows for as many as 33,000 people, an eightfold increase in population. The fields south of town are being filled in with houses, and people who built on side roads in Spanish Valley now complain that others are building across the road and ruining the atmosphere. People who live in Castle Valley, just over a mountain range from Moab as the crow flies, complain of light pollution from Moab.

The very worst case was presented in Stiles's satiric article on Moab in 2020, which may be the source of the now solidified rumor about Wal-Mart coming to San Juan County. Some boosters want an interstate highway built through the town, though it's not clear where it could go. Many people worry about development on the rim to the west of the town. Stiles talks of moving to western Australia to find the room he needs but concedes that things may not be as bad as he thinks, since many new people feel that Moab is a special place.

And the more of these people there are—up to a not clearly definable point—the better chance the atmosphere as well as the scenery can be preserved. Still, ironic contradictions between purpose and reality will continue to exist and probably multiply, like that in the public service announcement advocating a return to natural ways of living in Utah that used background music with a reggae beat and a reverb chamber.

TIGHT FIT IN THE JEMEZ VALLEY

Jemez Springs, New Mexico, has so much natural beauty that people have been drawn to it for centuries.

It is, or was, so remote that in 1942 Major John Dudley, in charge of site selection for a place to build the atomic bomb, decided that Jemez Springs would be suitable because it had a number of vacant buildings, few civilians would have to be evacuated, and "If the place blew up, only the six scientists would be involved and not all the families."

Of course, the village escaped that fate, but now it has to deal with problems caused by increasing numbers of people who pass through it and increasing numbers who want to stay.

For one thing, the village and the heavily used Santa Fe National Forest to the north are more accessible. Improvements in highways have cut from ten to thirty minutes from the fifty-mile trip from Albuquerque, and Albuquerque's suburbs are reaching closer every week.

For another, the federal government has created the Jemez National Recreation Area and will open, within two years, the nearly ninety-thousand-acre Valles Caldera National Preserve. The trustees are hearing suggestions for use, from hunters who want to close it every fall for elk season to city greens who, as Royce Tyler, a third-generation resident of the area puts it, want to close it to everyone except people eighteen to thirty-two who can hike fifty miles a day.

Whatever the trustees decide, Los Alamos covets the designation of gateway to the preserve, and most residents of Jemez Springs hope that it succeeds, but Los Alamos is a long and congested way around from the south—and, one resident says, some people won't drive through Los Alamos because of its associations with the atomic bomb.

Part of the problem is that, while some of the trustees seem to understand the new problems that the Valles Caldera will bring to the Jemez Valley, other agencies, county, state, and federal, seem clueless. William De Buys, head of the trust, had to ask the Sandoval County commission for a place on the agenda to talk about plans that will certainly affect the county. A representative for the Federal Highway Administration, touring Highway 126 to consider plans for paving it, did not know that it had been designated part of a National Scenic Byway and therefore required certain features to guarantee access.

All of that new traffic, like that currently estimated, some say grossly overestimated, from 1.8 to 3 million cars a year, must funnel through the village. Bruce Crozier's Jemez Area Residents Association Report (www.jemez.com/jara has a wealth of information) cites highway department surveys as showing under five percent growth per year for the past five years, under four percent over eight years, to about 2,000 vehicles a day. The official view is that a road like Highway 4 can handle ten times that many. This ignores the fact that less than forty feet separate the retaining wall of Los Ojos restaurant and saloon and the porch of Deb's Deli at the center of the village. The rest of the village center hasn't much more room. The state has rights to twenty-four feet of that, lip to lip of the paved surface—the only paved street in town. A bypass is inconceivable because the land slopes rapidly up to the mesas, National Forest land, on each side.

The traffic annoys different villagers for different reasons. Ordinary residents say that it goes through too often, especially on weekends, and too fast—and the numerous traffic tickets barely pay the cost of people to write them or to offset the regional reputation as a speed trap. Merchants complain that most drivers, called recreational tourists as opposed to those who stay in the local b&bs, don't stop to buy anything except bags of ice to take to mountain camps. And both groups realize that more tourists mean more emergency services for car wrecks and hiking disasters that federal and state governments don't pay enough to cover.

The people who live here and want to live here face other problems. Jemez Springs was designated an All-American City in 1995, but the 2000 census showed a decrease of nine percent to 375, and a far greater decrease from the 1998 estimate of 499.

On the other hand, the population of the valley seems to be growing. Since very little land is available in the village itself, people are building on the relatively scarce private land to the north and south. No head count has been taken, but over the past five years library membership has increased from 200 to 790.

The newcomers have made changes in quality as well as quantity. Older residents, some of whose families had lived in the area for generations, mostly ranched, cut timber, worked for the Forest Service or one of the three religious retreats (two Catholic, one Buddhist), or did what they could. Hispanics were in the majority. The area was rural, agricultural, remote.

Over the past ten years or so, people attracted by the incomparable scenery and the relaxed atmosphere have moved here to retire, to work as artists and writers (Rudolfo Anaya and Scott Momaday live here part time; Rollie Grandobis has exhibited sculpture worldwide) and, increasingly, in online enterprises, and to enjoy the atmosphere when they aren't commuting to the Los Alamos labs forty miles away or to Albuquerque. But as Bruce Crozier puts it, beginning about ten years ago, a series of new residents bought and rehabilitated old businesses, like three of the restaurants and two or three inns; some built new bed and breakfasts more luxurious than anything the village had seen before. New residents leased the Bath House, restored it, and now give out a thousand brochures a month, have thirty hits a day on their website, and, judging from the cars parked outside, a continuous flow of clients. (Trouble in paradise: after some controversy about the lease, the village government now manages it.)

Some residents, new and old, often put together various part-time jobs. Librarian Judith Isaacs says that she supports her "library habit" by publishing and selling a Jemez Valley cookbook, freelance editing, and teaching two online writing courses for a community college in Washington state. Diane Parrett, village clerk, is a certified clinical herbalist. Pat Bond, now court clerk, worked in the Jemez Springs bathhouse when she first moved here, and Ricca Gachupin Van Landingham, born and raised in the valley community of Ponderosa, returned to a job at Deb's Deli when she went for lunch and was snagged to go back to work. She lives at the Jemez Pueblo with her husband, who commutes to Bernalillo to work in the Hyatt Regency resort. But as Bruce Crozier says, no one moves to the Jemez for a job.

Most of the newcomers tend to be Anglo, urban in background, and better educated than the original locals, some of whom complain that these people come because they like the place and immediately want to change it. Some residents, and not just long-term ones, complain that the increasing number of homeowners who weekend and vacation here treat the place like a motel. A few were upset when the local bi-monthly newspaper, the *Jemez Thunder* (www.jemez.com/news), printed excerpts from a novel by local writer Linda Sweet, a twenty-year resident, that dealt with pre-marital sex and other abominations and ran a photo of a thong-clad skater on Venice Beach.

Outsiders have a different kind of culture shock. Shopping requires a good deal of planning. To the north, Los Alamos has the closest gas stations, and until the Jemez Pueblo opened its station at the end of March, 2001, to great celebration, San Ysidro, seventeen miles south, was the other option. Shopping for groceries and most other necessities requires a trip to Los Alamos or Rio Rancho.

Some changes are welcome. Kathleen Wiegner, editor of the *Thunder*, has a Ph.D., moved from Los Angeles ten years ago, and lives in a metal house of space-age design. She and her partners are committed to preserving the local culture and environment, but she welcomes changes like the availability of pizza and video rentals and the opportunity to get medical care any weekday rather than just twice a week. And she applauds the efforts of recent arrivals to establish a concert series.

But few people want major changes. Village officials would like more revenue to provide services, but members of the Planning and Zoning Commission agree, in a draft purpose statement, that "the rural, agricultural, historical and cultural character of the village" must be preserved and if possible improved. Judy Cunningham, a member of the commission, a landscape architect, and a refugee from development in Aspen and Estes Park, is most vocal about preservation, but her colleagues seem to support her views.

Of course, some residents resist any move toward regulation. A hearing on an animal control ordinance met resistance from people who don't have any animals. The planning commission agreed that there needed to be "Control and abate[ment of] unsightly use of buildings or land" and immediately listed the people who would complain. After the winter runoff and before the summer monsoon, the village water supply, which comes from springs, is low enough that people on hilltops are left high and dry, but though the village has permits to drill wells, residents insist on having spring water.

Still, the character of the village will change. Polly Westrick, manager of the local credit union, says that older residents are moving closer to medical facilities, and Realtor Doug Lewis agrees. (This seems to be borne out by figures at the community center, where lunches for seniors and others were down by about half in the first third of 2001.) Property is scarce, and it gets more expensive because outsiders pay what locals regard as outrageous prices. Lewis, whose real estate office, founded thirty years ago, was the first in the valley, says that in the early seventies lots just north of the village sold for $900. Now, depending on size, they sell for $35,000 to $40,000. Part of the increase he attributes to the increasing number of Realtors, for the higher the listing, the more likely one is to get the business. Californians are blamed for the increase, but Mary Carson of Oso Realty says that newcomers are more likely to be Texans or midwesterners, and Lewis thinks that most of the increase is due to people from Albuquerque wanting weekend cabins or camping space.

The local credit union has prospered as a result of higher real estate prices, increased services, increased visibility in a handsome new building, and inflation. Assets have gone from $300,000 in 1978 to $4 million ten years ago to $9 million in 2001.

Some residents worry about property taxes. Fears that taking the Valles Caldera off the rolls are apparently unfounded, since the federal government is paying Sandoval County ten times what the private interests were assessed, a fact that, one resident says, county officials don't want to discuss. But houses costing as much as $1 million are being constructed and older property goes for higher and higher prices, and that will in time raise other valuations. Long-time residents worry that their children will have to leave the area because they cannot find places to live or adequate jobs.

No one seems to be happy about the public schools. A number of people home school or send their children to private schools in Albuquerque or the Indian School in Santa Fe. New administrators are trying to make changes, including a program that allows a combination of regular and home schooling, but they have a difficult task both in the school and with public perception.

Despite complaints and worries, the infrastructure seems to be in good shape. True, getting a phone line can take six months and a complaint to the public utilities commission, but a government grant for a new sewage treatment plant means adequate service for a long time, and electricity is not only plentiful but, since the affiliation of the Jemez Mountains Electric Cooperative with Tri-State in Denver, bills have gone down seventeen percent. Of course, since the village has no paid maintenance help, the (unpaid) mayor had to go into the city, buy a part, and fix the library toilet.

More important for the general quality of life, the atmosphere of the village remains relaxed and friendly even by southwestern standards. Most people seem to reject calls for censorship of the *Thunder*. Most of the religious groups seem to co-exist peacefully, and the Fr. Fitzgerald Retreat and Renewal Center, run by the Servants of the Paraclete before the facility was turned over to the Handmaids of the Precious Blood, hosted not just Catholics but Presbyterians, Buddhists, and any group whose and purposes accorded with the center's character. Bruce Crozier, head of the Jemez Area Resident Association, attributes the atmosphere to the valley's long tradition of multiculturalism, where Indian and Hispanic sheepherders mixed with Lebanese merchants and Anglo timbermen and miners and so on.

There is a little eye-rolling about the tendency of some of the increasing number of New Agers to scatter crystals and feathers over sacred Indian and Hispanic sites or to burn sage and chant when viewing real estate, but there is no active discrimination like that at Tesuque Pueblo on the other side of the Jemez Mountains, where New Age merchandise is banned from the flea market.

But mostly old and new residents get along. Mayor John Garcia says that he belongs to both camps: he was born and raised here, left for thirty-seven years in the Air Force and civil service, and returned. He sees a decline in the "Us/Them" mentality, and cites the number of volunteers who donate equipment, goods, and labor for a variety of projects. Robert Borden, a partner in the *Thunder,* says that the whole valley "skates on volunteers" and points to the vital role of new residents, especially to the north of the village. Donations to the library overflow the shelves and spill into a metal shed that serves as the only real bookstore in Jemez Springs.

There are some worries. The Servants of the Paraclete own large parcels of land in the village, the order has dwindled to about thirty priests worldwide, and as with other religious orders, there are few recruits. If the numbers fall too low, residents fear that the property could be sold, and there is no guarantee that new owners would be as devoted to the culture and atmosphere of the area as the Servants have been. (Now the Handmaids have taken over, and that worry is eased for now.) On the other hand, the National Forest and the very conservative Zia and Jemez Pueblos (i.e., no casinos) in all four directions offer a buffer against outside encroachment.

There is also the possibility that increasing traffic, environmental problems, forest fires, and other disasters could make the area less attractive, as Bruce Crozier says, to baby boomers like him and his wife. But, as Royce Tyler says from his lofty position eleven hundred feet above the village, the people of Jemez Springs seem to enjoy worrying. And it is true that fears of McDonald's, Wal-Mart, and various franchised businesses seem unfounded, given the limits that available land and water put on any conceivable permanent population growth and even the wildest estimates of increased tourism. Doug Lewis thinks that the Valles Caldera will bring increased traffic only if it is part of the national forest rather than, as is currently mandated, a working ranch. And he estimates that paving Highway 126 will take, at present levels of funding, fifteen to twenty years.

Most of the residents interviewed, new and old, from Seattle, Massachusetts, Oklahoma, or the South Pole, have a strong loyalty to the place. As one said, after living all over the country looking for a place where she belonged, she recognized that this was home. But Susan Fitch-Mueller, who works at the post office and serves on the Planning and Zoning Commission, did have one caution: "Don't make us sound *too* good." On the other hand, Doug Lewis says to describe things accurately—while insisting that residents need to help prepare for changes that are sure to come.

BORDERS

SLOVAKIA AND OKLAHOMA

Officials in mid-sized American cities are fond of making alliances with "sister cities" in other parts of the world, especially those about the same size and having similar economic bases, perhaps as an excuse for traveling abroad. Prescott, Arizona, even has a sign at its edge giving the distance to its relative as well as to more easily attainable towns within the state.

European countries seem more disposed to draw analogies between themselves and American states. Most English-speaking Hungarians, for example, know that their country is about the size of the state of Indiana.

Perhaps I was influenced by this habit of comparison when, having been invited to Slovakia, I began to look for analogies with Oklahoma, where I lived for more than thirty years.

At first, the results were disappointing. Oklahoma has more than 3.5 times the area of Slovakia, which in turn has more than six times the population density—not to speak of real mountains. Oklahoma has a considerable Czech population, even a town called Prague, though the "a" is pronounced long. Another town, Yukon, calls itself the Czech capital of Oklahoma and has an annual kolache festival. But there seem to be no Slovaks—not that most Oklahomans could tell the difference.

Like many travelers, I found that my research taught me as much about my home territory as it did about my destination. The official almanac of Oklahoma reveals that we have an official song (from the Rodgers and Hammerstein musical comedy named after the state), an official country and western song ("Faded Love"), fish, game bird, regular bird, furbearer, reptile, beverage, meal (guaranteed to raise cholesterol levels), insect, motto ("Labor omnia vincit"), and flower. That flower is mistletoe, a parasitic plant—a symbol that must give a sour kind of cheer to the American Indians overrun by white Oklahomans.

This passion for labeling things to identify the state may come from the fact that Oklahoma has no clear identity. With few exceptions, every group in the state immigrated no earlier than the nineteenth century. Even the largest tribes of American Indians were deported to the area from their native lands to the east, and the white pioneers who did not sneak into Indian Territory sooner than they should have (thus the nickname "Sooner State," an odd thing to boast of) came in a series of land runs—races by hordes of settlers eager to claim "free" land formerly designated for use by the Indians.

In contrast, the Slovaks have dwelt in their homeland for more than a millennium, and although they have an official language and of course birds, insects, reptiles, and so on, these are allowed to fly, slither, or roam unburdened by official stamps of approval.

But these differences are superficial. Spiritually, Slovaks and Oklahomans have much in common. For one thing, both areas were for much of their histories regarded as colonies, outlying regions in large empires. Of course, Slovaks had a culture that was prevented from developing, and Oklahoma was empty land, at least in the view of whites, that had no culture in any meaningful sense. And even after Oklahoma was ninety percent filled with white immigrants, it could not be assigned to a specific region. One geopolitical map in the almanac assigns the eastern parts of the state to the South or Deep South or Ozark Region, the northern part to the Midwest, and the central and western part to the West. Or, as some observers put it more simply, "The men think they are in the West, and the women think they are in the South." John Wayne v. Scarlett O'Hara, in short. Slovakia may have regions, but at least the whole country has a definite place in Central Europe.

Modern inhabitants of both states are modest to the point of embarrassment. When I moved to Oklahoma from California, my students wanted to know, in as delicate a way as possible, what I had done to deserve this exile. Years later, a visiting dignitary from Hollywood was concerned about possible hecklers. "Oh, no," I said, "Oklahomans are touchingly grateful when outsiders show any sort of interest in them."

There are obvious reasons for this feeling of diffidence among both groups. A Slovak intellectual told me that the Hungarian word for "Slovak" has the connotation of "underdog," and in a dictionary of disparaging epithets in various languages, "Buda Toth" is translated as "Stupid Slovak."

In America, the equivalent word is "Okie," made famous but not created in John Steinbeck's novel *The Grapes of Wrath*. I even heard the word used by a Slovak radio announcer. Originally a short form of "Oklahoman," during the Dust Bowl of the 1930s it was applied to the only white American group of refugees to mean someone who was ignorant, dirty, poor, and generally a nuisance and a reproach to American ideals of prosperity and progress. One governor of Oklahoma tried to refurbish the term as an acronym meaning something like "OKlahoman Industry and Energy," but nobody, especially Oklahomans, believed that—or the legend formerly printed on all automobile license plates, "Oklahoma is OK."

Slovakia and Oklahoma occupy similar cultural positions. One Slovak intellectual maintains that Slovaks get their literary culture third hand—in Czech translations—and that while Czechs go to Paris, London, and New York to keep in touch with the latest developments, Slovaks are content to go to Prague. The separation of Czech and Slovak Republics has apparently not altered the situation.

Oklahomans are on the whole less interested in any form of culture—or that may be another example of Okie self-deprecation—but they also look to a larger city in a neighboring state. In their case, it is Dallas, Texas. The place of Dallas in the Oklahoma imagination is revealed in the remark by an Oklahoma judge that something was so obvious that it was "bigger than Dallas!" Oklahomans go to Dallas less for culture (though intellectuals have to travel there to see foreign films) than for the shopping.

Except for the Ukraine, Slovakia is surrounded by more prosperous and traditionally more self-confident neighbors, several of whom exercised political and linguistic hegemony over it. Oklahoma is more happily situated, for the state of Arkansas to the east is objectively poorer and mythically at least—Oklahoma's equivalent of the Ukraine—more ignorant and backward even than Oklahoma. (At least its former governor, Bill Clinton, is reputed to be sexually active. That cannot be said of any recent governor of Oklahoma—power is not *that* great an aphrodisiac.) Oklahoma shares very short borders with Missouri and New Mexico and a long one with Kansas, but the first and last do not figure at all in Oklahoma mythology and the second is regarded as a kind of Valhalla, not as a serious rival or destination.

But this respective superiority and inconscience are offset by Oklahoma's obsession with Texas, which borders it entirely to the south and almost entirely to the west. No matter how bad Oklahoma's economy or how many games our largest university's football team loses, a victory over the University of Texas is supposed to justify every Oklahoman's existence.

In some ways, Slovaks are more fortunate than Oklahomans. True, both have to learn new ways of speaking to communicate with the outside world, but Slovak is a perfectly respectable language with a literature and a history. And a Slovak speaking English with an accent will probably be regarded as both clever and charming. Oklahomans have not a language but a dialect that to the outsider, or rather the listener whose territory the Oklahoman visits, sounds comic and backward rather than exotic. They can understand us, but they listen not to what we say but to how oddly we say it.

Example: a colleague from New York, son of a famous literary critic, was new to Oklahoma. He mentioned something to me in a casual, elliptical fashion. I replied in a way that indicated not only that I understood his point but had moved on to the next stage. He looked at me oddly and said, "I'd have to explain that to most people."

"Just because I talk funny," I replied, "doesn't mean I'm stupid." I'm still not sure that he got the point.

Another example: I was visiting my son, who lives just across the Hudson River from Manhattan. Between us, we have five university degrees and have traveled widely. At a store, the clerk could hardly take his order because she was so bemused at the way we talked.

But over time, this comes to seem a minor annoyance, perhaps because Oklahomans get used to it, even expect it, and finally learn to make jokes about ourselves. And in the long run, regional and dialectical prejudice has not kept Oklahomans from moving successfully in the supposedly more sophisticated outside world. I hope that this is also true for Slovaks.

Still, it is pleasant for an Oklahoman to travel to a part of the world where people don't know the stereotypes about Oklahoma. Or, if they are aware of them, they don't care. Or, if they care, they can sympathize.

OKLAHOMA BORDER LINE

Although in the more than thirty years I lived and wrote in Oklahoma I was never actually stopped at the Red River and asked to document my right to enter Texas, I have the sense that invisible customs inspectors are waiting every time I try to bring my writing with me or ship it over the border. The varying signals take the form of submission guidelines that insist that the author be a bona fide Texan or at least hint that work by others will be scrutinized and possibly turned back. I feel like a tourist bringing back too much tequila from Juarez: I either have to dump the stuff or swallow it on the spot.

There are exceptions or variances, depending on who you are and what you seek to import. The *Concho River Review* puts no restrictions on poetry, though it prefers fiction to be "primarily [by] Texas writers and writers of the Southwest generally." The editors don't care about subject or mode in nonfiction, but "if the author is not a Texas resident, the piece should be about a Texas topic."

Not all magazines published in Texas are this restrictive, though I've never been able to smuggle a personal essay into a Baja Oklahoma table of contents. But even if every print medium in the Lone Star State had signed the equivalent of the NAFTA treaty, I'd still feel as unwelcome as a trucker with a load of Mexican strawberries. That's because no matter how much time I spend in Texas—and I'm writing the first draft of this piece in Fort Worth, Cowtown USA—I am not, never have been, and will never be a Texas writer even if I move there.

It's odd that I should even think about it. I don't think about not being a Kansas or a Missouri writer, even though I was born in the first, where I've never published any creative work, and raised in the second, where I've never published anything at all but am regarded in Boonville as a home boy because of a book I wrote about the town.

Nor, despite the fact that I've spent over ninety percent of my writing life in Norman, Oklahoma, do I consider myself an Oklahoma writer. That's not just because of gut-level snobbery. The real reason is that there *are* no Oklahoma writers.

At least not white ones—or, more precisely, those who are not Indians. Oklahoma was one of the first places in the country in which it was *chic* to be Indian—the politically incorrect local term used by everyone in the state, including what elsewhere would be called Native American. Joy Harjo, Linda Hogan, Scott Momaday, Lance Henson, Hanay Geogimah, and Geary Hobson are known to have Oklahoma connections, though only Hobson lives in the state, he wasn't born there, came there far more recently than I, and talks periodically about moving to Arkansas or New Mexico.

As a result, some very pale writers claim membership in the largest tribe of all, the Wannabes. The most striking example of self-initiation came at an "Oklahoma Poets Day" where, contrary to what you might expect, a lot of people turned up. The most memorable line came from a Latvian woman who declared that, having spent twenty years in Oklahoma, she regarded herself as an Indian. Some large Cherokees in the back of the room rocked ominously but didn't get up. I guess they figured, "What the hell, what does one more matter?"

She may have been inaccurate, even insensitive, but she had the right instincts. To warp a cold war saying, better red—or r-e-a-d—than dead. Nobody of any other color is regarded as Oklahoman, including Ralph Ellison, who was not only born and raised in Oklahoma City but wrote extensively about the state's cultural influence on his development as thinker and writer, or Tony Hillerman, who was raised in rural Oklahoma and set his first novel in Oklahoma City. How many white writers from Oklahoma can any but the most fanatical specialist name? Lynn Riggs? For every thousand people who have seen Rodgers and Hammerstein's *Oklahoma!* or every million who have heard the score, perhaps one knows that Riggs wrote *Green Grow the Lilacs,* the play on which the musical is based. And he was part Indian before it was fashionable, for all the good it does his posthumous reputation.

I can't name many more Oklahoma writers, and two I can name are also publishers. Frank Parman of Point Riders Press, now in his sixties, devotes much of his time to encouraging his contemporaries and juniors and to doing research about the activities of his elders. But Frank has just cut back on publishing. Susan Smith Nash of Texture Press, thirty years younger, takes a consciously international and avant-garde position, and has pretty much moved beyond publishing. Frank and Susan are natives. Other writers, like George Economou and Rochelle Owens, are in but not of Oklahoma despite having lived there for fifteen years. Same with me.

This leads back to the question raised earlier: "Why does it matter?" Does anyone worry about being or for that matter not being a Kansas or Missouri or Wisconsin or Illinois writer? (Maybe California writers worry; New York ones almost certainly do.) I've lived in these states without feeling or perceiving authorial *angst* about neighboring states. Writers there worry a great deal, but at least they worry on a national scale.

A second, related question is, "Why should Oklahoma be any different?" The obvious answer to this clearly rhetorical question is the neighbor to the south, looming over Oklahoma and its residents like a sow over the litter's runt. We have to keep an eye on Texas because we're afraid of being squashed.

And usually we are, and not just in letters. Not long after I came to Oklahoma, the latest in a long series of new university presidents commissioned an artisan to fashion a mace to be carried before him in academic processions and then revealed the object with considerable fanfare. Not long afterward, I passed a display case in the Undergraduate Library of the University of Texas and saw twenty-eight maces, one for the president and every dean on campus. In other words, we're in the position of East Germans before the Berlin Wall crumbled: those bastards on the other side have more of *everything* than we do, and no matter how hard we try to maintain that quality or purity or whatever is more important than mere quantity, we know that we're whistling in the dark.

144

That applies to just about every basis of comparison between the two states. Frank Parman says that Austin alone has more publishers of poetry than Oklahoma has practicing poets. According to the 1997–98 edition of *The International Directory of Little Magazines and Small Presses*, Oklahoma has sixteen publishers, and only one, Council Oaks, even attempts to produce books that have a professional look. Texas has seventy-seven.

And when it comes to literary magazines, the situation is even worse. *The International Directory* lists ten Oklahoma magazines. *Nimrod* has pretensions to international status and *Cimarron Review* to at least national status. *Westworld*, at Southwestern Oklahoma State University (not listed in the *Directory*), is regional. The University of Oklahoma sponsors *World Literature Today*, but no magazine that publishes work by American writers, let alone regional ones. Before Susan Smith Nash put *texture* on hiatus, the magazine was determinedly international.

The International Directory lists sixty-three magazines published in Texas—even more magazines than the University of Texas has maces: *Southwest Review* at Southern Methodist University, *Descant* at Texas Christian University, *RE: Arts and Letters* at Stephen F. Austin State University, *Southwestern American Literature* at Texas State University, *Concho River Review* at Angelo State, *Texas Review* at Sam Houston State, *Short Story*—at least the real editing—at University of Texas at Brownsville, *American Literary Review* at the University of North Texas. And there are dozens of more or less freestanding, independent magazines in the state.

Oklahoma does have a Center for Poets and Writers, which was located at the University of Oklahoma before moving back to Tulsa and a sounder financial base. It was "established to recognize the contributions of the region's [specifically not the state's] professional writing community and to provide opportunities for aspiring writers." The former seems to be taken care of by the center's sponsorship of the Oklahoma Professional Writers Hall of Fame, which until recently focused primarily on writers of genre fiction; the second is handled primarily by a Celebration of Books, mostly panels and speakers talking about their work, mostly in the popular/commercial line, and presumably giving advice.

The center is fairly new, and its mission and governance—who decides whom to honor and why—are evolving. But the director, Teresa Miller, realizes that a heavy mix of popular writers and writers from outside Oklahoma can be useful, even necessary, in calling attention to serious work being done by home-grown writers.

Oklahoma also gets badly outmaced by Texas when it comes to literary prizes. The Oklahoma Book Awards are sponsored by the Oklahoma Center for the Book, administered out of the Oklahoma Department of Libraries, with a governing board that lists three writers out of twenty-four members. It gives five annual awards— fiction, nonfiction, poetry, children/young adult (any genre), and design/illustration. To be considered for the award, books "must have been written by an author who resides or who has resided in Oklahoma, or have an Oklahoma based theme."

The Texas Institute of Letters, membership by invitation only, gives eleven awards, totaling over $18,000 and ranging from $250 to $6,000, including book of fiction, first book of fiction, nonfiction book, "book making the most significant contribution to knowledge," book of poetry, translated book, short story, children's book, book design, work of journalism in magazine or Sunday supplement, work of journalism in a daily newspaper. It's just as well that Oklahoma doesn't have the last two categories. Eligibility requirements are a little stiffer than Oklahoma's: "birth in Texas or two years' consecutive residence."

Texas has another type of support for writers. The month of May is devoted to Texas writers. Laura Bush, trained as a librarian, was the force behind the Texas Book Festival. The Dallas Museum of Arts sponsors Arts and Letters Live. "Texas Bound," readings of "Texas fiction interpreted by Texas actors," is sponsored by the *Dallas Morning News* with a foundation grant and support from various other businesses and foundations, and Southern Methodist University Press has published two volumes including forty-one of the stories read in the series. It is inconceivable that the *Daily Oklahoman*—the closest equivalent north of the Red River—would give that kind of support to any art, least of all to one as contrary and potentially subversive as literature, though it does have a pale imitation of the *News's* book section or the *Fort Worth Star-Telegram's* double-page spread that occasionally lumps together short reviews under a headline reading "Oklahoma Authors."

But Oklahoma has no equivalent of *Texas Books in Review,* published by the Center for the Study of the Southwest at Texas State, or

Review of Texas Books, published at Lamar University. Neither of these will be confused with nationally recognized venues, but the reviews tend to be more extensive and, though they make little attempt to reach beyond the book or author being discussed to place either in a larger context, they are for the most part more searching than reviews in the state newspapers' book supplement pages and at the very least provide news about and descriptions of new books by and about Texas. Furthermore, *Texas Books in Review* runs regular news about writers compiled by a staff of regional editors, so that readers and writers have a sense not only of work in progress and completed but of an ongoing literary culture.

Most of the books covered in *Texas Books in Review* are the kind that an Oklahoma equivalent, if it existed, could easily review: authors with varying intensities of local connection—ranging from the nationally known, like Larry McMurtry, Kinky Friedman, and Elmer Kelton, to the less famous, like James Hoggard, LaVerne Harrell Clark, and Marshall Terry—and topics equivalent to the Texas Rangers, horned lizards, and Hispanic murals in El Paso. Of course, the Oklahoma version might have trouble filling more than one issue unless it dealt with genre fiction, especially romances, at which Oklahoma writers seem particularly adept.

But one book reviewed in the Fall 1997 issue of *Texas Books in Review* is not and probably would never be possible in Oklahoma: *Texas Short Stories,* fifty-four of them, edited by Billy Bob Hill and issued in Dallas by Browder Springs Publishing. Even more astonishing is another collection, *Texas Short Stories: A World in Itself,* published in Fort Worth by ALE Publishing Company, a collection of twenty-one previously unpublished stories by Texas authors, seventeen of whom are, relatively speaking, from the hinterlands.

Let's get over the shock at finding that someone named Billy Bob Hill can read, let alone edit, and deal with the more interesting question of why such a book could not exist in an Oklahoma version. Even assuming that one could find that many writers of quality fiction who still live in Oklahoma—and that's not impossible—it is highly improbable that a publisher could be found and even more improbable that such a book would find a market. Only three newspapers would probably review it, and a few others might run the publisher's release. But there would be no serious discussion of the strengths and shortcomings of the collection or the individual pieces.

An earlier collection, Don Graham's *South by Southwest: 24 Stories from Modern Texas* published between 1940 and the mid-1980s, was issued by the University of Texas Press. It is barely conceivable that the University of Oklahoma Press would consider an analogous collection, though the editors seem more interested in nineteenth-century soldiers and Indians of any period than in work by the state's writers. But again, could Oklahoma come up with a list of writers to equal William Goyen, William Humphrey, Paul Horgan, Vassar Miller, and a half-dozen equally competent but lesser-known writers? We'll never know unless someone tries, and it is exceedingly unlikely that this will happen.

Oklahoma does not lack writers—I see a half-dozen promising ones every year in my workshops, and Frank Parman and others could come up with a much longer list over a cup of coffee—but as I have implied, by contrast with Texas it does suffer from the lack of a literary culture. That's not merely a question of relative size or relative wealth, the easiest excuse. Mississippi has terrible poverty and a horrendous literacy rate, but it has a healthy atmosphere for writers. So does Louisiana. Alabama, next to Mississippi geographically and in many other ways, doesn't.

It would be simple to say that Mississippi's literary atmosphere is anchored by major writers like Faulkner and Welty and well-known ones like John Grisham or that Texas has Larry McMurtry and Larry L. King, and Elmer Kelton and Clay Reynolds and Robert Flynn and Carolyn Osborne and so on and on—all of them identifiable as Texas writers wherever they happen to be living. It's true that Oklahoma never really *had* Momaday and Berryman and Hillerman and the Indian women as writers in the way that Texas had their writers. The next question is "Why not?" And the answer seems obvious: the magazines and publishers and other kinds of encouragement do not exist, never have, for young writers—who have to leave the state, or ship their work ahead of them, even to get started.

Of course, this happens to Texas and Mississippi writers, too. For example, Donald Barthelme served a long apprenticeship in Houston, but to get where he wanted as a writer, he had to leave the state, and like many young men on the make, he left the provinces on his way to a place in a larger cultural context with a parting shot at the narrowness of his home. "It is frequently painful for a Texan to decide that he is not, after all, a cowboy," he wrote in 1960, adding that this role means that "certain important areas of thought and feeling are closed to him. . . ." Alluding to a Houston group that almost successfully imitated the Modern Jazz Quartet, he realized "how much I have missed hearing the Modern Jazz Quartet." This was, of course, years before he returned from New York to teach at the University of Houston, by which time he, the university, and the city had changed a good deal.

But even after the changes that have taken place, including the creation of a real Texas literary and artistic culture, there remains a further question: Is the Texas writer well served, finally, by having a relatively secure and comfortable atmosphere in which to write and publish? Or do Oklahomans, who have to scrabble and starve and ultimately lash the furniture to the truck and head for greener pastures, have to face the more difficult but perhaps healthier choice of making it on their own in the larger world?

In some odd ways, the situation of writers in Oklahoma may be like that of Central Europeans before the collapse of the evil empire in 1989. Some of them got state subsidies, and even when they didn't have to make compromises, they had to write in certain ways about certain subjects in order to satisfy their patrons. Those writers now felt to be more interesting had to publish in *samizdat*, a situation that gave them a sense of vocation and purity of purpose because the work itself and the vision it presented were the only possible rewards for their labors. Now that the Wall is down and the possibilities of financial gain have risen, can they work or, even more crucially, connect with their readers in the old precarious and productive ways?

The same thing may be true of Texas v. Oklahoma writers. Texas has a flourishing literary climate; Oklahoma doesn't. But does being a Texas writer involve submission to the unspoken dictates of an invisible ministry of culture? Judging from some of the essays in *Range Wars: Heated Debates, Sober Reflections, and Other Assessments of Texas Writing* (SMU, 1989), this seems likely. Most of the contributors are laudably free from what Tom Pilkington calls a "naïve, chauvinistic reaction." In fact, denigration, backbiting, factionalism, subregional name-calling, and general bitchiness—most of it funny as hell if one isn't the target—seem to dominate the tone of most of the essays, some of which deal with issues I've raised in greater detail.

One such issue deals not just with physical residence but fictional material, and leads to the larger question, framed in specific terms: Does a writer like Barthelme have an advantage over one like Larry McMurtry, who left Texas physically but not thematically?

Oklahoma writers don't face that choice because they don't have one. I'm thinking not just of writers like Susan Smith Nash, whose Oklahoma roots are often so indiscernible that readers in Paraguay are more comfortable with her work than those in Poteau, Oklahoma, but of those like the younger writer Joey Brown, whose stories are flavored by the geography, language, and attitude of her native state. Most of Joey's stories have been published outside of Oklahoma. Few people, and fewer Oklahomans, know anything about her work. In Texas, she would more readily find outlets for her work, an audience to receive it, and possibly even a local publisher to issue her stories.

But would she be better off? In the current lack of literary culture in Oklahoma, Joey can't use a kind of cultural shorthand to reach her audience, so that she has to create as well as to reflect a world— and an audience. That's hard. But if she wants to be more than a local writer, even though she seems comfortable in writing "local color," the straight and narrow path may be better for her and for the writers, if not the readers, of her native ground.

WHO MOURNS THE GEPIDS?

The question about the Gepids—the answer is "No one," but the reasons why are interesting—occurred to me as I drove through the Navajo Reservation in Arizona and New Mexico through incomparable scenery, a lot of history, and often uncomfortable knowledge about the present, much of it filtered through the novels of fellow Oklahomans, Tony Hillerman and Ron Querry. Their books and other sources touch on problems of the contemporary Navajo, but they are more noted for their celebration of the coherence of Navajo culture and the sense of *hozho*, of oneness with the beauty of the world. This theme is attractive to many Anglos who buy into a nostalgia for a culture they don't know and who, as they learn more about Navajo-white relations, may not only feel guilty about overrunning other cultures but come to believe that these cultures are superior to our own. While this attitude is understandable, does credit to the goodheartedness of those who hold it, and is to a degree laudable, it is sometimes based on mistaken assumptions about or ignorance of human beings and the process of human history. More important, it can be a way of avoiding social and individual problems rather than dealing with them realistically.

Not that it's wrong to find Navajo country and its people attractive. The landscape is spectacular, and the human scene looks exotic to anyone who has not driven across other stretches of the American West. Scattered across the valleys and up gradual slopes to the mountains are ranches and farms, some with traditional hogans, some with modern, chiefly manufactured, housing, some with both, some with hogans that have two stories or ells. Here and there, small, dusty towns with wide streets, along which not many people move not very quickly. Except for the vernacular architecture, not all that different from West Texas.

Of course, it is different. The people here are darker and more heavily built and have a different lilt to their speech. And along the highways trudge a few pedestrians who don't bother to put out thumbs to the passing cars. Here and there a man or boy watches a pair of dogs herd sheep along or across the road. The core of the culture—what attracts the attention of outsiders who romanticize it—has not, despite missionaries of various sects, been fundamentally changed by Christian or European influences.

But those influences have been and are profound. The U.S. government's treatment of the Navajo, as of other Indians, is not pretty to contemplate: expropriation of land, deportation, fiddling with or outright breaking of treaties. Poverty and alcoholism rates are high. Educators struggle to keep the Navajo language alive, and there is a severe shortage of singers to conduct traditional ceremonies. No Anglo with any vestige of conscience can look at all of this without feeling guilty about what our people have done.

But we feel this way because we know what happened and is happening. And that brings me back to the Gepids and the question in the title. Few people in the United States or for that matter anywhere else ever heard of the Gepids or know that they were one of the tribes overrun and then obliterated by the Magyar incursion into the Carpathian Basin, much of which is now Hungary, a bit over a millennium ago.

Even those who have heard of the Gepids don't know much about them because, if they had a written culture, the Magyar did not, and thus would have had no means of recording and transmitting information in the unlikely event that they would have been interested. Thus there is no cult of Gepid spirituality or attempt to revive Gepid rituals or to uphold the Gepid way as superior to that of the people who displaced it.

In modern times, however, the winners have taken care, though not always the greatest care, to record information about the winning side, all the way from preservation, in translation, of the Aztec codex through Joseph Conrad's impressionistic account of European incursions into the Congo in *Heart of Darkness* to the latest self-styled white shaman's version of Native American culture.

Moreover, many contemporary marginalized cultures have representatives able to speak for them. Chinua Achebe, a leading African novelist, attacked Conrad for presenting issues from the European perspective. N. Scott Momaday speaks and writes eloquently about the culture of his forbears and other tribes. And this process continues, as in Geary Hobson's *The Last of the Ofos*, in which the sole survivor of a Louisiana tribe recounts the conditions that he has survived and, in the moving last chapter, speaks the language that only he knows to the wind and swamp. Among my own ancestors and distant cousins, Celts and Confederates have published whole libraries celebrating those ways of living and of interpreting the world. Celebrating one's heritage is not only honorable but necessary.

Of course, these apologists frequently attempt not simply to record ways of living but assert quite loudly their spiritual and aesthetic superiority to those of victors who depended on brute technology or accident—stirrups in the case of the Magyar; horses, steel, guns, and disease in the case of the Europeans who came to the Americas. The sins of their fathers are conveniently thrown in the memory hole—partly because people defeated thoroughly enough give themselves, and frequently get, amnesty for actions which, had they been performed by Europeans, would be roundly condemned.

Claims for the superiority of marginalized cultures are sometimes honored by defectors from the majority culture, the more sensitive or disgruntled heirs of the victors, for several reasons. For one thing, the hearers are impressed by the testimony of those who have special knowledge of their conditions. But Barbara Ryan, an expert in cultural studies, distinguishes between two kinds of testimony: the evangelical, which by its nature is a monologue and has significance merely because the bearer of witness says it, and the forensic, which is subject to questioning, corroboration, and rules of evidence. Many members of the majority culture are reluctant to consider the testimony of minority speakers in the second way, making the unconscious assumption that their status somehow gives their statements the stamp of infallibility.

These well-intentioned members of the majority have another reason for accepting criticism of their society: they can see that what victory has produced is far from perfect and coherent. On the other hand, a beleaguered minority group can seem more tightly knit and coherent than the culture from which the observer comes. Even as a lapsed Catholic, though not Irish, I found the hair on the back of my neck rising when I saw my first Orange Lodge. Later, while the Communists were discouraging if not actively oppressing the Church in Hungary, I bought a rosary from an old woman sitting outside the Pest Parish Church as a minimal gesture of solidarity. Those more deeply involved can be unified by outside pressure, like various Indian tribes who in previous centuries hated, despised, and made war on each other. Those who have never heard a Chero-kee talk about Kiowas or vice versa, to take one of many examples, might envy Indian unity in contrast to the divisions he or she perceives in white society.

Less supportable, at least without forensic examination of the testimony, is the claim that what has been displaced or suppressed is superior to one's own culture. Still, it is easy to understand how some people are able to think so. For one thing, a little knowledge can be consoling, and a lot of knowledge can be disheartening. We know a great deal about our own society and, unless we are experts, very little about others. Thus D. H. Lawrence could suppose in the absence of any hard evidence that the Etruscans had a culture far more balanced and harmonious than that of the vulgar, expansion-ist Romans who supplanted them and, of course, of the far more vulgar and expansionist society in which he lived. And, according to an anthropologist friend, many students enter her introductory course with highly romantic views of any people who can be termed "primitive." The Mayans were once considered to be gentle human-ists superior to the Aztecs, who had a highly developed civilization but also practiced human sacrifice, because, thanks to a Spanish friar, we have known something about the Aztecs for a long time. But until recently, when linguists like David Kelley were able to translate Mayan glyphs, we knew very little about the Mayans. It turns out that they skinned captives alive, among other things, and what they did when a king died will make you grab your crotch protectively.

There is also selective use of evidence. In *Legends of the American Desert,* Alex Shoumatoff has the "impression that most Navajo, even progressives who live in the cities of the Southwest, still live by the Navajo Way," which, he quotes a woman as defining, is "being in harmony with everything—yourself, mainly, all the living things, the air, Father sky, moon, and on and on." Wouldn't it be pretty to think so. But elsewhere Shoumatoff gives figures that suggest otherwise: "five hundred intoxicated Indians freeze to death or are hit by cars in New Mexico every year," and in broader terms, alcohol-related deaths, unemployment, tuberculosis, suicide, and infant mortality rates are much higher than in the rest of the population. Some of the problems are due to Anglo incursion or neglect, and they ought to be corrected as soon as possible. But it does no good to insist that the traditional system is perfect or necessarily superior to other ways of looking at life when it has so obviously failed to deal with these issues.

A second reason for preferring other cultures to one's own is the assumption that, because the people are not like us in some ways, they must be totally different. One example of this attitude can be seen in historical museums, where spectators and even curators seem fascinated by the possibility that primitive peoples created social structures and artifacts not wholly unrecognizable to the people on the other side of the glass in the display case. But for the most part observers tend to see so-called exotic peoples as wholly other and to regard as pure and unmixed their motives and responses. This purity is hard to discover in lived experience. Consider religious rituals. One might ask, though people rarely do, whether even the most traditional Hopis or Navajos are so much different from white Christians that they never have doubts about the efficacy of their rituals or sigh at having to get up and perform a ceremony or show up because it's expected of them or enjoy shaking their booty or wish to be somewhere else? Did all participants have equal faith and fervor? Did no one come for social or aesthetic reasons?

My experience tells me otherwise. During my college years, when I was a practicing Catholic, trying to observe not only the letter but the spirit of the law, I spent weekday mornings one summer vacation singing Requiem Masses at the parish church with two other college students. I can't speak to their motives, but mine were minimally spiritual. Ideally, the Masses were supposed to help spring the departed from Purgatory. But my decision to get up very early, before going to work, was primarily aesthetic rather than spiritual: I enjoyed singing, especially this kind of music, and there were very few aesthetic outlets in small-town Missouri in the early 1950s.

But at least I believed. A friend, son of a Texas Baptist minister, has lost his faith but not his taste for hymns, and he meets regularly with a group to perform "shape note" music, originally religious and now purely recreational. And many people seem to go to church because they can get out of the house, meet people, and engage in a different kind of ritual, like Shriners riding tiny motorcycles in parades.

It's possible, of course, that people we regard as exotic are really different from you and me. It's highly improbable that we can know. Outsiders like Tony Hillerman can imagine what it's like to be a Navajo in his mystery stories set on the reservation. Still, he hedges his bets by concentrating on Joe Leaphorn and Jim Chee, who have been to Anglo universities. And in any case, his novels deal with solving problems—whodunit—rather than with presenting problems, like alcoholism and alienation from the old ways, in their full complexity. The very nature of genre fiction distances the reader from these issues. This, by the way, does not make them bad books, but as Hillerman says, "My readers are buying a mystery, not a tome of anthropology. . . . The name of the game is telling stories; no educational digressions allowed."

Nevertheless, Hillerman, like every sensitive student of another culture, performs a valuable service in making readers more aware of the problems of a culture obviously under attack. And no one in the majority should regret attempts to preserve knowledge about other beliefs and ways of life. But no outsider, no matter how well-intentioned, should be allowed to forget Werner Heisenberg's uncertainty principle: one cannot study a phenomenon without somehow affecting it. Like ecotourism, which has much the same effect on an environment as the supposedly more vulgar kind, contact with other cultures affects them. To put it another way: consider the

Prime Directive in the original *Star Trek*. If Kirk and the crew of the Enterprise had observed it, at least half of the episodes could never have existed.

But many people who sentimentalize extinct or suppressed cultures do so less out of love for them than out of distaste for their own. Susan Smith Nash, a poet, translator, and cultural commentator who has worked with indigenous writers and who read an earlier version of this essay, sees the process as becoming "a sort of commodification of history that works because it scandalized certain behaviors (thus fetishizing them and titillating the audience), and it makes history (or the construction of it) an artifice to be retooled each season so that it's a fashion statement as well. Sentimentalizing is a kind of sales pitch—what's being sold? The thrill of voyeuristically contemplating atrocities? A way to appear enlightened?" Or, as a Navajo put it to Shoumatoff, "You Americans are looking for instant religious satisfaction, like instant mashed potatoes." In other words, like Lawrence with the Etruscans, the Other provides convenient and all too easy weapons with which to attack the ways of their parents, literal or figurative, in the dominant culture.

But in cooler and more logical terms, it seems unwise to regard the ways of other cultures as necessarily superior. Take the example of the film *Koyaanisqatsi,* the title a Hopi word meaning "life out of balance," which indicts America's rampant urbanism and mindless embracing of technology. That is a valid point—but to make it Godfrey Reggio used a number of advanced technological resources, and the review for the Internet's Apollo website concludes that "to get the full effect on video, you'll need a big screen, an excellent sound system, and the audio turned up good and high." Another online reviewer, Vladimir Zelevinsky, was left "with the feeling of elation and triumph. The sheer complexity of the urban activity and power and variety of humanity on display is enough to make one proud to be a part of these extravagant species [*sic*]."

This was a more eloquent version of my reaction to the film, and it leads to a broader issue: don't be too quick to despise the familiar. There is plenty wrong with modern American civilization and with Catholicism. But there is also a great deal to celebrate, for the traditions and rituals of both are rich and complex. And there is plenty wrong with colonialism, which Joseph Conrad's Marlow defines as "the taking it away from those who have a different complexion or slightly flatter noses than ourselves." As he says, it's not a pretty sight.

But it is a common one. Human beings are nothing if not opportunistic. Those to whom we did it almost certainly did it to someone else. My Celtic ancestors moved, or sometimes were moved, through Europe until they ran against the Atlantic Ocean. The Navajos and Apaches moved from western Canada to the American Southwest, where they harassed and, when possible, despoiled the Pueblo and other neighboring tribes, who helped in Kit Carson's campaign against them. The Apaches were forced farther south and west by the incursion of the Comanches. In the anthropologist's version, American Indians came from Asia. If one insists on tribal origin stories, the Navajos came up from a lower world to this one, specially created for them. That, and the Navajos' name for themselves, Dineh, The People, sounds a little like Manifest Destiny. Or consider the case of the Kennewick Man, whose remains, nine millennia old and not indisputably Mongoloid, were discovered in Washington state. Scientists want to test the DNA; Indian groups maintain that this is intrusive and that, since he was discovered on their land, he must be Indian. In any case, they argue, they have always been here, so he has to be one of their ancestors. There is every reason to respect native culture and traditions, but imagine what the response would be to similar claims by white Christian fundamentalists, including the Kansas textbook board that removed textbooks that so much as mention evolution.

But the Indian claim points to a serious question: which people can be called indigenous? While I was drafting this essay, I heard a talk by a learned and earnest young Osage scholar who listed a number of indigenous peoples in the Americas, Australia, New Zealand, and Africa. With the exception of the Lapps—and perhaps the Basques, they might argue—Europe apparently has no indigenous peoples. But the term really means that no one knows when they got where they are now.

I raise this issue not to quibble and certainly not to justify regarding any other culture as inferior or to excuse some or even most of the actions of those who moved in, including Euro-Americans. Nor to make my fellow Americans feel triumphant: our turn will come.

When it does, those of us who survive may take whatever consolation is possible in the sight of the disaffected heirs of our conquerors, whatever their color, affecting the outward and visible signs of our culture. Perhaps really avant-garde youth will wear three-piece suits; drink Chivas Regal; dine at ethnic restaurants serving meat loaf, mashed potatoes, and green beans boiled limp; listen to Lawrence Welk and Neil Diamond; and attend re-creations of tent revivals. They may even hire us as gurus and tour guides.

In the meantime, it might be well to follow the advice of the strongest character in Frank Chin's novel *Donald Duk* to a boy who hates being Chinese: "History is war, not sport." And like Donald Duk, you have to learn about your history in order to celebrate and defend it. And about others' histories in order to counterattack. True, the Navajo were overrun, decimated, and treated shamefully. But what had they done that made other tribes attack them when Kit Carson began his campaign?

Actually, this kind of knowledge is most useful in dealing with European critics, as when they claim that jazz is a purely African invention. One can reply, without denigrating the major influence of a host of black geniuses, sung and unsung, that of course they based their innovations on traditional African instruments like the cornet and play songs like "Strutting with Some Barbecue," which is obviously based on traditional African forms like the march. More serious and more frequent is the charge made by Europeans that America is a violent nation. I have to agree: we have too many guns, too many deaths, too much hate. But then I tell them about a visit to a synagogue in Szeged in southern Hungary. It was large, ornate, beautiful. But there weren't any Jews. Then I invite my antagonists to compare body counts for the two continents over the past century.

A friend tells an even more pointed story of an American in China who was confronted about his reaction to some idiotic decision made by his president. He didn't agree with it, he said, and he had written the president to tell him so. End of discussion.

But this kind of thing is mere skirmishing. We also have to deal with internal critics who attempt to deconstruct American history and institutions. Some of this is necessary: the George Washington cherry tree type of history persists in the minds of many Americans, including those who infest the editorial page of the largest newspaper in Oklahoma. All we can say to these criticisms is "Yes."

And then "but." The young Osage scholar speaks of a responsibility to his own past, his own family, his own history. We have the same responsibility, made more difficult by the greater burden of knowledge and the even greater burden of success. It can be tempting, as Geary Hobson points out in "The Rise of the White Shaman as a New Version of Cultural Imperialism," to shirk this burden and try to become a reverse image of what blacks, Indians, and Asians call Oreos, apples, bananas—white only on the outside, red, black, or yellow on the inside. This kind of distortion makes the imitator ludicrous in the eyes of the people being imitated. As Hobson says, people like this need "to restore themselves to their own houses— by learning and accepting their own history and culture."

That doesn't mean that any of us can afford to ignore, let alone despise, other cultures. The Osage hasn't cut himself off from white language and culture; Frank Chin knows about Westerns and flamenco; Ralph Ellison knew about Hemingway and Malraux and a whole lot else; and Hobson, a Quapaw-Cherokee-Chickasaw, teaches Faulkner. But none of them wants to be an imitation white man, and it would be equally mistaken for whites to try to be Navajos or blacks or anything else but what we are. And what we are is in part a heritage, a family, and a history, and none of us can escape these, or should try. As King Duk says in Chin's novel, "You gotta keep the history yourself or lose it forever. . . . That's the mandate of heaven." Shoumatoff quotes the Navajo phrase about "becoming real"—getting rid of false values and seeing the true nature of things. All of us need, Chin would agree, to take responsibility for what we have become and will become. Perhaps Shoumatoff should consider more directly that there are ways, besides the Navajo way, of doing so. Owen Wister, perhaps a little too obsessed with his white heritage and values, nevertheless has a point when his Virginian insists that there is only one kind of goodness and that he tries to follow it. "And when I meet it," he adds, "I respect it." And so should every Asian American, African American, Navajo, and anyone else who hopes to become real—by whatever name it is called and whatever process it is attained.

AS GOOD AS A MYTH

NOT IN KANSAS

Although I know, of course, that I was born in Lyons, Kansas, I no longer think about it much except when the information is required for an official document. Otherwise, when asked where I'm from, I shuffle through a list and usually come up with Missouri, where I lived from the ages of four to nineteen and where my siblings still live.

I had very dim memories of Kansas, like a series of snapshots: my standing outside a display window in Coffeyville while my mother rushed up to find her errant son; playing on a dirt street and climbing on a vacant chicken house behind a rented house in Arkansas City; cutting a thumb on a tin can and learning left from right with the scar as a guide.

But during most of my years in Boonville, I thought of myself as a Kansan because I was born there, my parents grew up and met there and told semimythical stories about their childhoods and families and showed me photographs of mysterious people, places, and events like the dust storm that cut the photo in two as if half had been exposed to the light. Also, I had numerous cousins there, and my maternal grandfather had a modest place in local folklore. Mostly, though, I did so because Kansas was not Boonville, Missouri, and that allowed me to distance myself from an environment that I frequently thought boring, restrictive, and even hostile, especially to those newly come to the area.

This attempt to discover or invent more exotic or distinguished origins was rather like the apparently common childhood fantasy— one I didn't cultivate—of being adopted into a family far less distinguished or exotic than the original one. Or perhaps it was like the popular culture superheroes in the comics I read in which the superhero was disguised by an undistinguished public identity.

Most of the time I didn't insist on my origins, though I did root for the University of Kansas against the University of Missouri, only twenty-five miles to the east. Partly this was native patriotism; partly, like my rooting for the Brooklyn Dodgers over the St. Louis Cardinals, it was a way of separating myself from the crowd and perhaps of being annoying at the same time.

When I went to college in Kansas City, on the Missouri side, I was so busy trying to overcome the prejudice against my outstate accent and manners and to construct, with however vague or unconscious a purpose, a new identity as a cosmopolitan intellectual that I didn't have time to think about my Kansas background.

Nor did I think of it much when, after graduation, I went to a reporter's job in Great Bend, thirty-one miles west of Lyons. This was a poor choice for someone with my aspirations. Great Bend was more than twice as large as Boonville, but I didn't know anyone there, the hours were long, and in any case I didn't have much time to think about my identity. Once, gathering material about high school football teams in the region, I actually went to Lyons without any curiosity. Otherwise, I stayed on the highway of a flat, dull-looking town half the size of Boonville as I passed through it on my way to Hutchinson or Kansas City or, the last time for forty years, to Lawrence to enter the graduate program at the University of Kansas.

The rigors of those two years left me little time to think about my identity or origins because I had to concentrate on my future. Besides, on the rare occasions when I looked up from books and typewriter, Lawrence seemed, in contrast to Kansas City, as dull and provincial as Boonville, though it is probable that I was more dull and limited than my surroundings.

In any case, my two years in Kansas burned out my fantasy of being a native. When asked where I was from, I could use the MA from KU to establish a temporary professional identity until I got a

Ph.D. from the University of Wisconsin. No one seemed to care about more remote and personal origins.

Later, when I moved to Oklahoma, Kansas was merely a place to drive through as quickly as possible because, except for the Flint Hills, there seemed to be nothing to delight the eye or engage the mind as I drove up I-35 through Wichita, Emporia, and smaller towns to visit my relatives in Missouri. Once, visiting an aunt in Sedan, I left the interstate and drove through Arkansas City, conscious of the family myth but too busy or incurious or immersed in my own continuing saga to stop and look around what seemed a pleasant but rather ordinary town.

And the journeys got longer and more extended, to places where people couldn't distinguish Kansas from Missouri or anyplace else in the middle of the United States. On one of these, I began to think about the years I'd spent in Boonville and, over a period of seven years when I spent more time in Hungary than I did in my nominal home town, wrote about and became reconciled to the experience.

A few years later, after a sharp romantic disappointment, I headed north from Oklahoma, which I didn't and don't think of as home after thirty years, to Salina and west toward Denver, alone, feeling sorry for myself, and searching for whatever kind of anchorage I could find. Passing the Arkansas City exit, I thought of my forbears, now living only in the facts and myths of their lives and stories— mostly, because I am the oldest survivor with the most tenacious mind of my generation, in my memory.

At Wichita it was time to leave the familiar freeway that veered north and east toward Missouri for one that would lead me west. It runs straight through Wichita, where some of my numerous cousins live, shorter, more sedentary if not always more stable, who share a sense of humor and a past two generations back. Thinking of them, I can see, as in a distorting mirror, various lives I might have led.

Except for the massed ranks of grain elevators, there's nothing much to see from I-135. But that day I spotted, white against the grey concrete, two egrets standing placidly in the drainage ditch that runs between the north- and south-bound lanes. Like me, they were displaced, but they seemed content on the unfamiliar surface.

North of Wichita my only memories were of a hurried previous trip toward a certain destination. None of my family had lived there, but in my free-floating state I liked to think that the people had lives as regular and even as their fields. Flat but not empty; not introspective or emotional. Perhaps it was the geometry in the angles of fence and windbreak that led me to think so.

At Salina, west on I-70, hoping to see the West open out. I wouldn't pass through Lyons, but I knew it was there, to the south, another alternate life. My parents had no relatives or friends there; only some anecdotes about dust storms and a goat whose milk cured my eczema, and perhaps some photographs without labels tied the family to the town.

North, where I was driving that day, the land began to open out. Geometry was behind me. Here the landscape was more rounded, with a few trees nestled in cracks and folds to punctuate the curves, almost female. *Memo to God: You're the one drawing the dirty pictures.* Still, there was a pattern, dictated by geology rather than by man-drawn lines.

But the West didn't open out as much as I'd hoped. The TV had forecast a cool front, and westward the air thickened.

And West is different here from the one I've seen on so many trips across I-40, several hundred miles to the south. Here the billboards seem less boisterous. One for a roadside zoo, but almost no regional souvenirs for sale. One touching in its desperation: "Next Exit - Pioneer Village, Minden, NE. 132 mi. North. Open every day all year." The Czech capital of Kansas, with an opera house and museum. "Shaw's Homemade Sausage in Downtown Wilson." Campus Road—what campus? "See the largest prairie dog in the world." Nothing more exotic than I'd find in Oklahoma or Missouri; nothing to stir the imagination.

Until I passed the Cathedral of the Plains, St. Fidelis Church, at Victoria, where a colony of Germans absorbed the town named by feckless Englishmen.

Fidelis. Faithful. I grew up in a German Catholic community, or subcommunity, and descend, through my mother's mother, from one farther east that, through all her wanderings with my grandfather into Kansas, Missouri, Indiana, Missouri again, she never really left. Solid, hard-working, practical people, faithful because, I sometimes thought, they could imagine no alternative. Bound by lines, like the people whose land I'd traversed 150 miles past. No

Deutschland über alles for the feckless English and Celts who had diluted my mother's mother's blood.

No signs of or about Indians, even faked. My younger colleagues, intoxicated by French theory, use terms like "erasure." It fits here: European migration, Swede, Czech, German, have blotted out the names of tribes I do not know. The migrants were not exterminators, though they followed the dream that led to extinction. How guilty are they? How guilty were the Comanche who drove the Apache west or the Kiowa who thrust their way onto the plains? How much guilt did I inherit from the ancestor, perhaps collateral, the not-at-all-feckless Englishman who came to Virginia three centuries ago and was called the "Apostle to the Indians"? People move. Some of them stay. Is that worse or better than moving on as I have done from Kansas and everywhere else?

Meanwhile, signs if not symbols: a water tower in the middle of nowhere. A stone house, not built on sand, but abandoned in the middle of a field. The mind tries to create patterns through allusions, correspondences, whatever will work. Amy Lowell's only memorable line: "Christ, what are patterns for?" What are they for? We need them: kinship, marriage, love. Security. Something to hold on to.

That day, like many days, my only pattern lay in the AAA Trip-Tik. The land grew harsh and flatter. Road signs and what they promised, signifier and signified, appeared almost simultaneously. With language unnecessary, the mind flattens out.

On the trip back, this time not alone, I hear tales of another's Kansas: marriage, motherhood, betrayal, moving on. An impulse: go back thirty, sixty years.

Great Bend was not difficult to navigate, at least to the newspaper office where I worked, a block from the courthouse. The newsroom, once next to the presses, had moved upstairs, the receptionist said. Did I want to see it? No. Other technologies; another life. The twenty-year-old reporter, skinny and unsure, I could not find there, though he lurks on the fringes of my mind.

On to Lyons. Asking for the hospital—the only point of reference I could think of—I was directed to the one west of town. No, I said, the hospital that would have been used in 1934. Oh, that's a few blocks south and east.

It wasn't hard to find: a two-story brick building that looked a little like the school I attended. But the sign said "Glass Menage," a whimsical allusion I hadn't expected on these scruffy plains. No one was visible, and I didn't care enough to approach the building to learn what the current inhabitants did there. Any karma from my birth was long dissipated.

So, finally, was my sense of being a Kansan, except technically. I had gone back, but back was no longer, had never really been, home. For years, it had been the somewhere else to which I could imagine escaping from wherever I happened to be. The desire had not changed. But in the harsh summer light of central Kansas, the magic dissipated. It will form, has formed, over places more conventionally exotic. But never again Kansas.

THE ORNAMENTAL HERMIT

Always remember: no matter where
you go, there you are.
Buckaroo Banzai

A friend of mine who moved from West Hollywood to Jemez
Springs, New Mexico, mentioned that in the eighteenth century it
was fashionable for wealthy people to build a hermitage on their
estates, hire an ornamental hermit to inhabit it, and take their guests
out to see the picturesque result.

It is possible to construct psycho-social and even sexual theories
to explain this phenomenon as a kinky way of allowing the inhabitants of the Age of Reason to feel guilty about their opulent lives and
get an extra kick at the same time, rather like the sybarites who
chained a starving slave next to the banquet table. In *English
Eccentrics,* Edith Sitwell attributes the fad to the desire "to escape the
consequences of being alive."

But it is dangerous to feel superior because, though our factories
are rusting, we are part of the same industrial age, and while no one
hires a hermit anymore, society as a whole supports people like
Thoreau and Edward Abbey.

Neo-transcendentalists and Greens will resent this label and
insist that these men were not hermits but prophets. I don't think
so. True, a hermit leaves the world from disgust or in search of a personal vision; a prophet may look like a hermit (cf. John the Baptist—
locusts, wild honey, skin of beasts, the whole hermit bit) but comes
back to the world to demand that people change their ways, for the
day of the Lord is at hand and evil-doers will be smitten.

169

But there is an important difference between a prophet and an ornamental hermit. A prophet pisses people off so badly that he pays heavy dues. (I'm using the masculine pronoun because in Judeo-Christianity these roles have been male-dominated, but women have increasingly begun to fill them.)

An ornamental hermit is a minor pain in the ass because he acts morally superior, though not enough to make people want to kill the messenger, and he has a much cushier deal. No nonsense about eating locusts or having ravens come to minister to him: the National Park Service brings him his food and water in the desert or he heads into town for a piece of Mrs. Emerson's pie. Any time he feels the need, he heads back to civilization to pick up his paycheck or his book royalties or whatever subsidy he's managed to work out. He has a lot of disposable time on his hands and either no life partner or a very tolerant one.

Best of all, he gets to astonish his friends by turning his back on civilization. He makes lists of the things he does without. He makes an inventory of how cheaply he lives. He is so close to nature that he becomes intimate with ants or snakes or whatever inhabits the vicinity. In the days before Aldous Huxley turned mystical, he made an apt comparison of "the modern professional sportsman [to] a certain type of Christian ascetic" and associated the latter not with humility but with "the will to power."

It is easy to become competitive about self-deprivation. My friend and I had a mild debate over which of us deserved the title, though first we agreed to waive the ornamental part. He has to go a mile or so up the road to pick up his mail. I have to drive twenty miles, climbing a thousand feet, then dropping two thousand, to get mine. He has a fax machine and cable TV; the public phone nearest to me is ten miles away, and I don't have a TV set. On the other hand, he made a permanent move to Jemez Springs from West Hollywood, while I am spending two months in Seven Springs during my summer break from teaching in Norman, Oklahoma.

Mere solitude doesn't get you any points. I've been by myself in a number of places, including ones where I couldn't speak the language, didn't have a telephone, and got mail much less frequently. But places like Halifax, Paris, and even Debrecen in eastern Hungary arouse envy rather than awe in one's friends. You have to be away from what people think of as civilization, and you have to seem to be depriving yourself.

It's tempting to overstate one's break from civilization. For example, my only source of heat—useful in the mornings, when the temperature is in the mid-40s—is a wood stove. But I'm writing this on a computer. I have indoor plumbing, a microwave oven, an automatic coffeepot, and gourmet coffee from the nearest store ten miles away. True, the washing machine is broken and my Instaplak tooth-care system has seized up from the minerals in the water, which is translucent but not transparent. The electricity is a little uncertain because of the mountain thunderstorms.

My friend in Jemez Springs isn't as isolated as I am up here, but our respective sets of friends are equally astonished. Visitors from LA wonder how he can stand the isolation and then sit on his porch and stare transfixed at the shifting light on the multicolored layers of the canyon wall. My writing students were so nonplussed at my plans that they didn't even know—except why in God's name I would want to do something like this—what questions to ask.

I even managed to astonish my sister, which is not easy. She grew up hearing me complain about having to live in a town of 6,000 people. When she and her husband came to visit me up here, they hit the end of blacktop several miles before they reached the cabin. She said, "*Bob* is living out here, alone, for two months?"

After thirty-seven years of teaching, I've learned to tell people what I think they can understand, so I told my students and my sister that I came up here to get away from the Oklahoma summer, force myself to go on a macrobiotic diet so I could get into most of my wardrobe, and finish drafts of two books, neither having a thing to do with my life up here.

Only the last goal required any concentration, and I accomplished it, as far as I can until I get to a library, with two weeks left to think about where I am and what it means besides allowing me to feel morally superior. That's pleasant but addictive, and as Frank Chin says in his commentary on Sun Tzu's *The Art of War*, "Don't start believing in your own bullshit."

But ornamental hermitism can be useful—mostly to the hermit, but also to society. Leisure is hard to come by, solitude harder, quiet harder still. They are no less valuable even—especially—if the hermit goes back down the hill because they allow one to pay attention to different things in a different way.

The most obvious difference between here and home is the landscape. Geology is always underfoot and always changing, and ecosystems everywhere respond to the slightest variations, but most people don't notice either unless dramatic differences hit them between the eyes. Here, in thirty miles, over a dirt road that changes from volcanic white rock to Permian red clay and back again and causes passing tourists to inquire plaintively about how far it is to pavement, ponderosa and aspen forest gives way to open meadows, then to a view across three mountain ranges, and finally to sagebrush semidesert. If you believe, as eighteenth-century rationalists did, that the proper study of mankind is man, then you do well to refuse, as Dr. Johnson did, to look at the Alps. I grew up in farming country, where nature can jerk you around, and have lived even longer in Oklahoma, where it can blow you away. But this country can just as soon kill you as not.

Some of the differences are more subtle but no less dramatic. From my window, I can see both the bank of the Rio Cebolla (sounds exotic; translates as wild onion creek) and the canyon wall. The vegetation of the two is entirely different: thistles and cow parsnip to the left; aspens above an almost geometric line to the right. Half-way up the logging road to the meadow behind the ridge, Indian paintbrush and drabber plants whose names I don't bother to learn make their first appearance.

Temporal as well as physical rhythms are more obvious. Morning comes late in the canyon, but the sky is pure turquoise. By lunchtime, clouds have moved over the ridge or down the valley, bringing rain and some thunder. At full dark, the skies are full of pin-sharp stars.

You have to learn the rhythm and adapt to it. Luckily, mornings are my writing time, when it's safe to turn on the computer, and I finish in time to get in an hour's walk before the noon storm and perhaps another in the evening if the clouds have passed over.

Because there is less to see and hear, the variations are easier to catch. My window looks down the valley to a sharp, wooded bluff, a view that reminds me of Monet's use of the cathedral at Rouen: interesting in itself, it is more interesting as a backdrop against which the changing light reveals itself in sun, twilight, or the almost too picturesque mist that forms over the stream after a thunderstorm. Sounds play against the backdrop of the stream—wind in the ponderosas, bird calls, a truck across the bridge, a weekend power mower.

The local fauna moves to its own rhythms. In two months, the flycatchers nesting over the porch light have laid and hatched their eggs and departed with their young. I miss their company. The robins and a host of other birds have also moved on, leaving the Stellar's Jays and hummingbirds in charge of the habitat. The stream of black ants in the kitchen gives way to hordes of large, noisy flies too big for the flycatchers to handle and then to fat, bold mice who demolish two boxes of D-Con in forty-eight hours. A sign of fall, says the woman at the High Country Store on the last day of July.

Most humans here are also transient, their habits as noticeable as those of the birds. (Not counting the weekend campers in the Santa Fe National Forest; there goes the neighborhood, say the cabin owners.) Every two weeks a new band of Texans arrives at the cabin across the dirt road. Almost every weekend the man two cabins up arrives with more materials for winterizing his cabin. In the early morning, he and I are the only people stirring, compulsive at our tools. (He drives to the nearest spring to get water for coffee because he uses cream, and the iron from his well turns it green.) Others are less regular, like the man in the next cabin who drives sixty miles, cuts his grass, and drives home as soon as he is finished.

It's easier to learn about the humans because everyone tells you about everyone else. I know how much the owner is asking for the place across the creek, how much he paid for it and to whom, and what the renovations were and what they cost him. I know how deep the well is and what further repairs will be necessary to make the place livable. I know why the posts that blocked the north end of my lane were set and when and why they were removed. I know who shot the hummingbird with a .45 and whose teenagers—now grown and gone, like the flycatchers—committed what atrocities. Some people know that on a previous visit I had a different companion, and on the theory that it is better to be offensive than defensive, I tell them that this was four years, three books, two women, and one computer ago.

The local metropolis, Jemez Springs, has about four hundred

more or less permanent residents, two churches, four restaurants, a library open two days a week and two Saturdays a month. Residents of Santa Fe resent intruders and refer to them as aliens. ("Don't let the aliens get you," a man muttered to me on the Plaza, apparently because I didn't look like a Californian.) In Jemez Springs, three visits to the same place makes you almost a regular. And with so many tourists needing directions, it's easy to sound like an old mountain hand.

Everyone knows everyone else because they have to. As my ex-Hollywood friend says, there's no twenty-four-hour repair service. Except for the Forest Service and the religious centers (two Catholic, one Buddhist), there are no regular sources of employment, and most people wear three or four hats, and not everyone has an office or even a telephone. The most reliable and fairest purveyor of firewood is a former Wall Street investment analyst who does archeology and disposes of rattlesnakes on the side. Or maybe this is two guys who do six other things between them. One Realtor is also a mechanic. The owner of the local bakery also manages security for the geothermal plant.

None wear as many hats as a rare year-round inhabitant of Seven Springs who lives, without water or electricity, in a cabin on the ridge whose materials he hauled up a precipitous path. He knows the qualities of all the local plants and everything that moves. He plows snow, hauls wood, clears brush, replaces floors and roofs, and cleans chimneys. I'm not sure that he can make shoes, but I wouldn't bet against it. On the other hand, a bowl of milk doesn't work—it takes at least a six-pack of beer. But he's a lot more versatile than the elves.

He lives according to the seasons: work in summer; hunt in autumn; read philosophy in winter; get in shape to work in spring. He's neither ornamental nor a real hermit: he works all over the region, and everyone knows him. And he repudiates attempts to make him into a special kind of person. "It's just work," he says.

One night my electricity went out, and it took me two hours to discover that it hadn't happened to everyone else in the area. My neighbor called the repair service, and by midnight the two-person team, one Anglo, one Hispanic, had very deftly put a new transformer in place. My neighbor watched every move and said, "You guys are the real heroes."

By the standard he sets, the ornamental hermit seems too much of a dilettante to be taken seriously. But he—and lately she—is not entirely ridiculous. We need to know that man is not the measure of all things—nor woman neither. It's best to learn it for ourselves, but being told is better than not learning it at all. The thing is not to be too superior or boring about it. Some of us make longer stops at the scenic areas than others, and some bring back technically superior records, but ornamental hermits are tourists, perhaps more socially conscious and less prone to littering than some, but no more permanent a part of the landscape.

DEATH IN THE WEST
A Multicultural Adventure

If you live long enough, sooner or later you're
gonna get into some really weird shit.
Scenes from the Class Struggle in Beverly Hills

I grabs me an armful and sorts through
it until I gets to the one with
the ball. Then I keeps him.
Big Daddy Lipscomb

He is dead! said Obadiah,—he is certainly
dead!—So am not I, said
the foolish scullion.
Tristram Shandy

In Frank Chin's first play, *The Chickencoop Chinaman,* the main
character opens the second act with a monologue about his childhood fantasy that the Lone Ranger was really Chinese: "he rode a
white horse named Silver cuz white be our color of death. Ha ha ha.
And he was lucky Chinaman vengeance on the West . . . and silver
bullets cuz death from a Chinaman is always expensive. Always
classy. Always famous."

It's dangerous to disagree with Frank Chin. Almost as dangerous
as it is to agree with him. So I'll do neither, but say that death in the
iconography of the West is always public. Think of the burial platform in *Little Big Man,* Jack Palance's lonely grave in *City Slickers,* the
fictional Boot Hill in *Shane* and the real one in Tombstone. Like
everything else between Lawrence, Kansas, and the Rocky Mountains, you can see death coming from a long way off.

West of the Rockies, the landscape is different but the concept is the same. In fact, the first book I ever read about Los Angeles (in order to write about it for the Catholic Community Library book review contest instead of doing a term paper in a Milton course) was Evelyn Waugh's *The Loved One*. As most people know, from the Tony Richardson movie that travestied it if not from the book, the novel contains a caricature of Forest Lawn Memorial Park just this side of libel—lawyers on both sides of the Atlantic checked before publication. At any rate, long before I was familiar with the idea of Avalon or the Hesperides, I knew that the West was closely tied to the idea of death. Aldous Huxley's *After Many a Summer Dies the Swan* and Nathanael West's *The Day of the Locust* did nothing to dispel this notion.

In 1991 I went to Los Angeles to work on a book about Waugh's visit in 1947 that provided the inspiration for his novel and the material for his article "Death in Hollywood," profusely illustrated in *Life*.

Waugh had been amused and shocked at Forest Lawn's parody of Christian, specifically Roman Catholic, eschatology, since Hubert Eaton had managed to abolish Judgment and Hell, muted Death as far as possible, and seemed to reduce Heaven to a cross between a playschool and a Rotary Club meeting. When I first visited the place, in the late 1970s, I did not have the impression that there was anything religious about the place, partly because an extended Catholic education had given me rigorous standards for the definition of that term.

But in 1991 I saw Forest Lawn through the eyes of a very different writer. Except for the fact that their chief object in life seems to be annoying people by being rude in very stylish ways, Evelyn Waugh and Frank Chin seem to have nothing in common. Waugh was a short, plump, white, upper-middle-class English convert to Catholicism who worked his way up to a country house and came eight thousand miles to see the place. Chin is a tall, thin, yellow, bohemian Chinese American pagan who seems to prefer being on the road somewhere between Los Angeles and Seattle and lives on the steepest street in Los Angeles not far from the original Forest Lawn Memorial Park in Glendale.

Frank had never visited the place until I lured him down the hill and up the gentler slopes of Forest Lawn with the promise of breakfast and a new experience. I don't know if he thought the place was religious, but he had no doubt that it was Christian. Sitting in the Great Mausoleum before the stained glass reproduction of "The Last Supper" as the curtains opened, he didn't quite manage to stifle moans that sounded something like "Whoa!" at the canned narration describing Leonardo's symbolism and touting the superior virtues of the replica. Our only common association with the scene was Mel Brooks's *History of the World, Part I*. Frank doesn't know much about the situation that occasioned the painting, and I made no connection between it and the complicated and impressive Holy Week ceremonies of the pre–Vatican II Catholic Church in which I had participated for years.

After the curtains closed and we walked to the car, Frank was uncharacteristically silent. Even on the way to the gift shop at the top of the hill, he had little to say, but he absolutely refused to enter the building that houses the huge paintings depicting Christ's Crucifixion and Resurrection. Since these were introduced long after Waugh's visit and since I know Frank well enough not to argue with him, I got in the car and headed downhill again.

We could not visit the Wee Kirk o' the Heather because a funeral was in progress, but we did get a look at the Church of the [Kipling's] Recessional before heading out. Frank summarized his impressions with "White people are even weirder than I thought," apparently and especially Christian white people.

I tried to convince him that real Christians (i.e., Catholics of the pre–Vatican II sort) were very different, and by telling him stories about saints chosen as patrons of various professions by the oddest kind of association (St. Lawrence, martyred on a griddle, is one of the patrons of cooks; St. Teresa of Avila is patron saint of headaches). He said that he kind of missed St. Christopher, who had been declared a non-person in one of the Vatican's attempts to impart historical accuracy to its hagiography. (My father, even more pagan at heart than Frank, never paid any attention and carried a St. Christopher medal in his billfold until he died.) Anyway, I almost managed to convince Frank that my brand of Christian was kind of interesting because these vignettes were almost as outrageous as some of the episodes of *The Water Margin* and other Chinese heroic tales. I didn't try to tell him about prayers for intercession with God or anything like that, partly because I didn't want to lose his attention and partly because I had forgotten. And it now occurs to me that Forest Lawn offended him less because it uses Christian iconography or even because it is relentlessly Eurocentric than because it is static: it doesn't tell any stories. Moreover, the most impressive or anyway the largest monuments come from someplace else and don't seem to have much to do with the landscape. Kind of like Charles Foster Kane's mansion, only less crowded and better ordered.

We still had most of the day before us, and he insisted on going someplace to clear our minds or at least give our imaginations something more interesting to work on: the Gene Autry Western Heritage Museum in Griffith Park.

There we were on common ground—the West of the two-for-a-dime Saturday afternoon movies, a never-never land where six-shooters fired innumerable rounds from an invisible banana clip, heroes fanned the hammer to shoot guns out of the hands of whole squads of bad guys or rolled around dusty streets and barrooms without ever getting dirty. Gunshot wounds were nearly invisible; those hit slumped gracefully to the ground or did acrobatic flips off balconies. Nobody important ever died. Gabby Hayes *was* old, but obviously he had always been that way. The cattle didn't go to the slaughterhouse, and no one ever had to clean out the stables.

The museum is a monument to that world: instead of relics, souvenirs you could get by sending in box tops; impossibly shiny guns; sheet music and record jackets celebrating singing cowboys—even, grudgingly, Roy Rogers, Gene's biggest rival in our youth—and all the rest of the paraphernalia of the B Westerns churned out by Republic Pictures and other minor studios.

The only signs of the real West—I'm talking about what I can remember, not writing a catalogue of the collection—were a Butterfield stage coach in showroom condition and a curving bar complete with cuspidors, which shone all the way to the inside bottom.

I'm not a stranger to the fake West—the National Cowboy Hall of Fame and Western Heritage Center in Oklahoma City has its share, including the carbine John Wayne carried in *Stagecoach* and the hat he wore in dozens of pictures. But at least the hat is batted and perforated, the carbine looks as though it had been used, and the largest piece in the museum, in its own building, is "The End of the Trail," which at least acknowledges that Indians existed. Some of the three-dimensional exhibits in the West of Yesteryear use real Western gear and, when called for, authentic dirt. Farther south, Fort Sill is still an active post with a real graveyard dating back more than a century, has a museum where the wheeled ordnance looks thoroughly used and the artillery pieces on Cannon Row came from real battlefields.

Frank knows the difference between the real West and the Gene Autry Western Heritage Museum as well as I know the difference between real Christianity and Forest Lawn, and in any case both of us, in our fifties, have lapsed from the faiths of our childhood. Had we ever really believed in Gene and Hoppy and Roy and their kind? At an obvious level, no. But it was nice to believe that good guys won without using excessive violence and didn't really have to *do* anything about the heroines. Still, both of us were now sobered by parodies of the real thing.

The oddest moment of the day was seeing a tall, upright, very elderly man being accompanied into the museum by a large and obviously important entourage. Could it be? Nah! Yes, by God, it *is* Clayton Moore, though he isn't wearing the costume or the mask he'd fought in court to wear.

In *After Many a Summer Dies the Swan* and *The Loved One,* Huxley and Waugh refer to Tennyson's poem "Tithonus," about the mortal, beloved by the dawn-goddess Aurora, who was granted eternal life but not eternal youth and "wither[ed] slowly in [her] arms, Here at the quiet limit of the world."

In Griffith Park, nobody's cowboy hat floats, but the vision of the Lone Ranger, aged and bereft of Jay Silverheels, told us that we had come to the end of a whole imaginative world. In a way the Gene Autry Western Heritage Museum is more depressing than Forest Lawn. At least it memorializes, with its deplorable improvements on great art and even more deplorable originals, people like Irving Thalberg who worked and struggled and sometimes created in the real world. The stained glass version of the West presented by the Gene Autry Western Heritage Museum had even less to do with the reality, past and present, than Forest Lawn does with the real cultural heritage of Europe, let alone the grimmer facts or even traditional Christian concepts of death. Both memorials are theme park versions of the real thing, and the trouble with theme parks is that they don't tell stories that go anywhere or mean anything. All art is selective, but real art isn't sanitized and bound by a reassuring paper strip.

Nathanael West was another outlander who wrote about Los Angeles (born Weinstein, he wasn't true West), and the passage from his *The Day of the Locust* is often quoted: "It is hard to laugh at the need for beauty and romance, no matter how tasteless, even horrible, the results of that are. But it is easy to sigh. Few things are sadder than the truly monstrous." West didn't have the chance to visit the Gene Autry Museum, and he didn't mention Forest Lawn.

Frank and I drove past the runners and cyclists on the shaded paths of Griffith Park and got back to reality, or whatever the freeway represents, where sighing is a luxury that no modern Angeleno can afford. By comparison, West's Los Angeles seems almost pastoral. Looking around him, Frank repeated what has become a refrain: "It gets more like *Blade Runner* every day."

It wasn't a bad line, but it didn't really fit. The sun was shining; there wasn't much smog; the people we'd seen were fairly relaxed and mostly Anglo. In fact, Frank was trying it out to see if it would work in whatever he was writing or would write.

In that movie, as in Huxley's *Ape and Essence,* where a Hollywood cemetery becomes a kind of archeological Wal-Mart for the degenerate natives, the lovers move north and east away from a culture that celebrates death to find a refuge, seeking an older idea of a West that provides green space and freedom. That too is a dream, at least as delusive as the one portrayed in Gene Autry's movies.

The real West, and the past it embodies, still lies between Frank's home and mine. Fenced, diminished, even despoiled, strip-mined by romantic novelists and revisionist historians, it doesn't seem a suitable arena for heroic action or heroic two-fisted writers. Jack London killed himself, and even Ken Kesey, who's older than Frank but, depressingly, a little younger than I, calmed down considerably.

In "The Middle Years," Henry James's Dencombe believed that "we work in the dark—we do what we can—we give what we have." But the modern writer, especially one oriented to the West, works in a harsh and unforgiving light, and a lot of us find it easy to blink or put on a rosy shade of a slightly more credible version of the Gene Autry West.

Some don't, though they move in mysterious ways. I dropped Frank at his condo to work in the light of his Mac screen and the television screen on a novel first titled "Gunga Road" and then *Gunga Din Highway*. He says he writes by arguing with CNN. I don't know how this accords with the wisdom of the mysterious East, or even east of Kipling's Suez, but it fits with the characteristics of Frank's personal patron, Kwan Kung, noisy god of writers and fighters.

I headed toward West Hollywood in search of material about a dead Englishman writing about death who is often as red-faced and angry as Frank's patron but is not likely to be canonized in either the traditional or modern senses.

Shrines are supposed to reinforce faith and induce spiritual calm. Forest Lawn and the Gene Autry Museum merely renewed the itch of old myths, which no longer satisfied but could not be shaken. Irritation probably doesn't fit poor Dencombe's view that "our doubt is our passion and our passion is our task. The rest is the madness of art." But at least it lets us know we're alive and pushing each other. And writing.

GENE AUTRY, OKLAHOMA
Different Slants

Natives of almost anyplace sooner or later realize that until they take visitors, they don't bother to see the sights. If they have bothered, they don't see them clearly until they have an outsider's perspective. I knew that Gene Autry, Oklahoma, existed—I'd passed the exit sign on Interstate 35 dozens of times on my way to Texas—but I didn't know that it had a museum or an annual music and film festival "Dedicated to the Singing Cowboys" until a colleague passed on a flyer sent by a friend in South Carolina.

Even then I wouldn't have considered going. But I mentioned it to Frank Chin because he has called himself the original Chinatown Cowboy and made the Lone Ranger a character in his first play. (The Masked Man turns out to be a white racist complaining that the Chinese American central figure put too much starch in his shirts and confesses to an affair with Helen Keller.) So when I told him about the festival, he said, "Wow! You've got to arrange to get me to Oklahoma." So I did.

Gene Autry, Oklahoma, our destination, got that name in 1941— it used to be Berwyn—because Autry owned a ranch in the area and the town fathers thought it would be good publicity to make the change. Thirty-five thousand people showed up, the most ever to crowd into the town limits. When we got there, the place seemed almost deserted, but Frank was fascinated.

I'm from two-lane blacktop territory, and I'm used to seeing villages along railroad tracks with a couple of stores and churches and houses scattered irregularly around. And a small-town school, like this one, across from the Baptist church, that holds, or held, all twelve grades and had not only an auditorium that probably used to be the gym where the stage is out of bounds at one end, or would be if they hadn't built a gym on the other side of what is now the post office. The auditorium was like the places where I'd played basketball in very small-town Missouri. There weren't anything like 35,000 people there; at most 200, and probably fewer, showed up that Friday.

I've been in enough small-town museums not to expect much—even from one supported "by those persons wishing to preserve the memories of the early western movies for their children and grandchildren," among whom I can't really be counted. What we got was a series of school rooms, desks removed and a very respectable collection of singing cowboy stuff inserted. One of the larger rooms was—is—a store, "The Blue Rooster," where you can buy collectibles, some new, some antique, or what people my age prefer to call classic, like Portuguese Gene Autry comic books, guns, games, and plastic guitars, one for $450, another from which Frank tried to wring some chords, left over from the heyday of the singing cowboy movies. There's a Gene Autry room—bed, furnishings, and all.

At the festival, there's lots to buy. Flanking two sides of the auditorium and three of the gym were tables full of stuff for sale: tapes and photos of the performers in the first, shrink-wrapped comics, Big Little Books, videotapes, cheaply made toys that now command, or anyway ask, big prices in the second.

More or less continuous music from auditorium and gym, more Nashville than the kind of stuff that Gene and Roy used to sing. Frank, an accomplished guitarist, says the performers aren't bad. No names that we recognize: Tex Hill, "the Rhinestone Ranger." Jerry Arnold, singing to a tape backup, who's at least sixty and made her first album in 1993, three thousand advance orders for the new one in production. She had a number one hit in England with "Living a Lie" and numbers three and six in Denmark and Germany. Paul Belanger, a winner of the National Jimmy Rogers (for Rodgers?) Yodeling and International Swiss Yodeling Championships. There's this whole subculture we never heard of.

But the most unusual feature for both Frank and me was the impersonators standing around in the halls and auditoriums. These were men dressed up to look like Hopalong Cassidy, John Wayne, either Gabby Hayes or Fuzzy Knight, Johnny Cash, Wild Bill Hickok, a few that neither of us can identify or who are going for the generic B Western look. Frank classifies the guns as real, fake, plastic. There's lots of piping on the costumes. There's not many places where grown men could wear this stuff without being laughed at or hit on, in the old or new senses of that phrase.

I found the sight vaguely embarrassing, like seeing your father in a funny paper hat, but Frank got more into the spirit than I or anyone else seemed comfortable with. Having got Hopalong Cassidy's autograph, Frank reflects, "This is the sunset, buckaroos. The Old West is getting dim. The old back's played out and the old lady is old. Owoooo! Hear that wolf?"

In fact, everybody at the festival looks fairly old, even by Frank's and my standards. Of course, it is a Friday morning, and respectable people are doing honest work or attending school, unlike this wandering pair of urban intellectuals. Sitting beside me on an auditorium bench, Frank surveys the crowd and says, "We're the youngest people here." And later, "You and I are the only colored people here."

Punch line from a joke heard fifty years ago: "What do you mean *we?*"

"I'm not doing this by myself," Frank says. "Besides, you're a lot more like me than you are like them."

Some of my Confederate ancestors might have been shocked at the first remark, but I took it as a compliment and even used it as an operating principle while we were there. As a result, I felt almost as alien to the proceedings as Frank did. We weren't made to feel unwelcome—in fact, though very few people at the festival had ever seen a six-foot, long-haired Chinaman with a moustache and shooter's glasses, they seemed more impressed that he had come all the way from Los Angeles and was familiar with the big Gene Autry Museum in Griffith Park. Norman, Oklahoma, apparently seemed only a little less exotic.

After lunch, there was a ceremony honoring Dick Jones—who'd been a child actor in *Mr. Smith Goes to Washington* and *Destry Rides Again* and dozens of other films as well as television series like *Buffalo Bill, Jr.* He's now selling real estate in California. Johnny Western introduced him. Johnny wanted to be Gene Autry when he grew up, and he did tour with him and later wrote the theme song for *Have Gun, Will Travel*. Now he's a d.j. in Wichita. Western provided an apostolic succession of singing cowboys: Will Rogers encouraged Gene, who encouraged Dick Jones, who encouraged Johnny. And there, I said to Frank, the line of succession ended, with Johnny Western the fit, tanned equivalent of the last member of a line of royal pretenders living out his days on the Riviera.

That was a little sad in a pleasant, non-threatening way, but my capacity for nostalgia is curbed by a good memory, and the singing cowboy movies had never really appealed to me even when I was ten and preferred more gunplay, less music, costumes that didn't have piping and glitter or checks, and hats that fell off and got dirty.

By late afternoon, we'd had as much nostalgia as we could stand. On the way back, and after, I wondered about how serious the performers and audience were. Was this like a geriatric Star Trek convention? Or did people come out of nostalgia rather than to escape to a totally invented world, though of course the B westerns were fantasy of a different kind? Later, both of us tried to write about our visit to Gene Autry, but neither was satisfied with the results.

Frank went on to other projects and I to other places, but the trip caused an itch that wouldn't go away, and I needed to see the museum from my own angle rather than Frank's. So in August of the next year, I pulled off the interstate and headed to Gene Autry again.

This time there were only three people in the museum—Elvin and Flo Sweeten, who founded the museum and manage it, and Willie Johnston, who keeps it going. There wouldn't have been a museum if the school hadn't closed for lack of students. The "Pop. 200" on the sign at the north side of town hadn't been true for years. I asked Elvin how many people lived there. "Ninety-two," he said. "No, ninety-one. Somebody died this week." Six students made up the graduating class of 1948, and there were only twenty-five in the whole high school, so state aid was cut in 1949. Now students are bused to nearby towns.

After the school closed, the building was occasionally vandalized, so people who had gone to school there boarded it up and kept and eye on it. Elvin had always wanted a museum, and Flo had always wanted to run a gift shop, and while they had liked cowboy movies as children, they hadn't remained enthusiasts or been collectors. But the town name gave them a convenient theme. So they put together a board of directors, which meets once a month for a covered dish dinner, opened the museum in 1990, and started a collection from scratch. Later they drafted Willie, who graduated from the high school in 1951, worked in an oil refinery for thirty-six years, and now does all the framing, cabinet work, and general troubleshooting.

The three of them keep the museum open seven days a week—all are now retired from their paying jobs—and average twenty-five to thirty visitors a day, in 1997 from twenty-seven states and three foreign countries. In 1991 they commissioned a fiftieth anniversary belt buckle, and ads for that put them in touch with people across the country. They started with Gene Autry memorabilia and then expanded it to the other singing cowboys. Elvin says that twenty-six actors tried to sing; six actually could. There are exhibits for musicians, like Spade Cooley, who don't seem to have played cowboy roles but dressed that way. Some of the memorabilia—five to ten percent—is donated; the rest they have bought across the country in various scouting expeditions.

Private donations from supporters in Ardmore helped them get started, and memberships, ranging from Saddle Pal ($25) to Hall of Honor ($500) keep the museum going. A Community Development Block Grant paid for reroofing the building and refurbishing and air conditioning the auditorium, which is also used as a community center, and they hope to air condition the rest of the building and maybe do something about the plumbing. They have a website and an e-mail address and plan to keep going and getting better.

They get some volunteer help at the annual festival, held in late September as close as they can get to Gene Autry's birthday, when the building could use air conditioning. The festival began in 1991 and, with a hiatus in 1992, has been a yearly event since. It draws as many as 1,500 people over three days.

The more I talked to Elvin and Willie (Flo was busy with customers or friends or both in the gift shop), the more clearly I realized that Frank had been wrong. I am at least as much like these people as I am like him. I was even surer when Jim Brock, who had been on stage with Gene on the big day of the name change, came in and talked about a funeral he'd just been to. "He didn't have any friends," Jim said, "but he did have two Purple Hearts." My father and his friends, or my brother and his, couldn't have delivered a more succinct epitaph.

None of my family would have thought of starting a museum, but they would understand the impulse that led Elvin and his friends to see a need and figure out ways to fill it with a lot of physical labor, some merchandising know-how, some salesmanship, and enough savvy to get a government grant. They have made something—not out of nothing, but, much harder, out of something that was about to crumble from lack of use. That's not exclusively western or even American, but it is an accomplishment for them to be proud of and for others to praise.

To understand just how wrong Frank had been about me, I had to go back to the festival to see it in a way other than as Frank's faithful Okie companion in the movie about him. (That's one of his favorite ways of looking at the world and one of the reasons it's so interesting.) This time I was in my own script as a small-town boy who had become a writer, additional dialogue by Elvin and Willie.

The crowd was old—older than I, probably, though there were some young people. But this time Frank wouldn't have had to draft me as an honorary colored person: there was a Hispanic-Indio couple named Melindez and later in the day what my father would have called a real colored person if he had been on his best behavior.

This was a Saturday, so the crowd was larger than last year's Friday crowd, and though I was the oldest person wearing running shoes and had one of the few beards, I looked and talked enough like the rest of the crowd to fit if not blend in. When people learned that I was there to write something about the festival, they were eager to talk to me, and some wished that they had thought to bring a tape recorder like mine.

Frank and I had missed the benefit auction in 1997, so I sat in on the 1998 version, cried in a green gimmie cap by Greg McMeans of McMeans Auction Company. I've been a fan of auctions since I used to walk to the sale barn near my house in the country and hear Colonel Patrick cry sales for cattle and mules. Greg was less dramatic but competent. The records went for prices ranging from $5 (an Eddie Arnold) to $30 (Gene's "Christmastime"). Janet McBride, one of the performers, who had taught LeAnn Rimes to yodel, got the only Elton Britt record I've ever seen for $17.50. A Roy Rogers twin-sized quilt brought $300, the three-stringed Gene Autry guitar from the gift shop $200, Gene's book *Back in the Saddle* $125, and a paint book $65. Princess Di and Erin Bear Beanie Babies—*Beanie Babies?*—brought $70 for the pair. But the big ticket items were new and hand-crafted. A fourteen-karat gold saddle ring with seven sapphires and four diamonds, made to benefit the auction, brought $525—well up from $325 for last year's version. And Gene Autry, OK, spurs, made in Mill Creek and raised high, like the golden calf in Exodus, brought $550. Applause at the sale of these, perhaps because the audience was impressed by the price, perhaps out of tribute to the craftsmen who had made and donated them.

Over in the gym, besides toys, comics, and a campaign poster for Jimmy Davis, when he ran for governor of Louisiana singing "You Are My Sunshine," there was a booth for Cowperson Tack that sold authentic-looking reproductions of Colts and other frontier weapons that sold for considerably less than the $125 asked for a toy pistol at another booth, though an 1880 Colt .45 was priced at $350. The whole family, three generations, does leather work, the seventeen-year-old grandson's gun belts and holsters the most spectacular if least useful for today's riders.

The look-alikes are there—Lash Larue, the Lone Ranger, Herb Jeffries, aka the Bronze Buckaroo, Fuzzy Knight are new this year. The Duke, Gabby, Hoppy are back. Johnny Cash didn't make it. This year they seem more human, perhaps because I'm circulating more freely. In the men's room, Hoppy asks Mickey Dawes, one of the performers, where he gets his suits with piping on them, and the two men go into a serious comparison of sources, like dowagers in Bloomingdale's. Later I hear Gabby asking Lash where he got his hat. Lash takes it off and reads the label.

Wandering up and down the halls, I see the Lone Ranger and Bronze Buckaroo posing for pictures—a real study in black and white. When the Buckaroo is free, I talk to him and discover that his name is Boyd Gunning, that in real life he drives a truck in Tennessee, and that he drove over for the festival. He used to dress up as the Lone Ranger, he says, but people kept pointing out that the Masked Man was white and besides, didn't wear a moustache. Boyd always shaved off his beard for festivals, but he clung to the moustache. Then a John Wayne look-alike turned him on to Herb Jeffries, who had a moustache and the right complexion, and he'd found his niche. He's in touch with Jeffries, divorced again and living with his son in California and accessible through his website. Jeffries has been invited to attend festivals, including this one, but Boyd says that he doesn't think he looks as good as he used to and refuses to appear in public.

I didn't ask Boyd why he does this, partly because it didn't come up and partly because I didn't want to pry. But clearly he enjoys getting out of his regular life, and like the other look-alikes, he is plugged into a regular circuit of festivals. Later I found that they come on their own, for this festival, at least, doesn't pay expenses. So it's obviously a labor of love—and if not love, they do get a fair amount of attention from people in the audience.

The performers were much more open about their motives. Many of them had retired from other jobs—several from law enforcement—in order to follow the circuit of festivals and concerts. I stopped and talked to Janet McBride, who was a deputy sheriff in Dallas County for eighteen years and ran the Mesquite Rodeo on the side. Now she's retired and singing all over the United States and Canada. In the lunchroom I sat with Ed Parker. He was a real cowboy before he started singing—a bull and bronc rider, then a calf roper and pick-up man in rodeos. He also did leather work, was sheriff of Orange County, Texas, worked in the oil patch, taught in a police academy, and had a part in a movie. He tried substitute teaching to see if he wanted to do that full time but decided that it was too tough. In 1983, he said, he was diagnosed with cancer and when he'd come out of treatment decided to do what he really wanted: be a country singer.

Mary Schutz, who performs with her husband Tex, used to do publicity for public television in Nebraska before retiring to the Rio Grande Valley and performing more or less full time. When she found out that I was writing about the festival, she went into her publicist mode and offered me tips and lots of information. Like many of her colleagues, she's unhappy about the current state of country music, especially the refusal of radio stations to play traditional artists and material. How long has it been since you've heard Hank, Senior or Junior, or Waylon? She and Tex wrote "Put the

Country Back in the Music," including lines like "If that's what comes from Nashville, then shame on Tennessee."

These and other performers have a whole circuit of venues and network of professional organizations that I and indeed most country and western fans have never heard of. Tex and Mary used to hit about ten of these each summer before they retired; now they go to about twenty, sometimes combining the swing with sight-seeing. This circuit of festivals, mostly in the Midwest, is a kind of substructure undergirding Nashville and Austin. Many of the festivals pay only the headliners; some pay expenses; some give free booth space where performers sell their tapes for a gross of $25 to $1,000. None of the performers at Gene Autry are stars, and their songs never get played on the radio. But they keep working. And delighting old audiences—and some new fans, like the graduate student from Spain I took to the festival on my fourth visit who became an instant celebrity and had her picture taken with the John Wayne look-alike to send to her mother.

The performers succeed because they are in close harmony with their audience. This was most obvious in a scene I came across just behind the registration desk after I paid my entrance fee. A tall man, Gary Hart, was standing in the hallway playing his guitar and singing "Wild Side of Life." Bill Craven, a smaller, leathery man carrying two guitar cases walked by, said, "I never heard *that* before," pulled out a guitar, and began to play. Ed Parker and Tex Schutz added their voices, and Mary came by and picked up the lyrics in mid-line. They were joined, sometimes only for a line or two, by paying members of the audience. Including me.

Later I realized two things. First, the performers come to the festivals not for the money but to keep performing—for and with each other. Second, the line of succession from Will to Gene to Dick Jones to Johnny Western, though it doesn't continue in movies or on television, has not been broken. These performers, with their directness and integrity, come out of a world I recognize and remember. But they're more like the singing cowboys than the people I grew up with, for they sing their songs and head over the horizon to the next festival, drifting like tumbleweeds, in new-found freedom.

THE MYTH OF A WEST

A friend who has lived in Ashland, Oregon, for more than twenty years remarked that she somehow doesn't feel that she is living in the West. Having spent a couple of days there, I said that this was because Ashland is like a stage set for a particularly good production of *Our Town*. It's clean, neat, cultured, quiet, and white. Also, of course, it is full of tourists come for the Oregon Shakespeare Festival and has more restaurants and boutiques and bed and breakfasts and ecology defense organizations per square foot than any town of comparable size west of the Mississippi. Or maybe anywhere.

On a drive to the Oregon coast, we decided to have breakfast on the road. On this Sunday, or maybe any other time, there wasn't anyplace to eat in Dillard, a lumber products town that lived off the clear-cut mountainsides we saw, but Winston had a restaurant with one or two spots left in the parking lot. My friend has come a long way from Bogalusa, Louisiana, in a different kind of timber country, and she remarked that the town and the patrons represented the Oregon that one could forget about in Ashland, the Oregon that elected Republicans and wanted to grill spotted owls for breakfast.

It was obvious that neither the clients nor the menu in this working-class town resembled in any way the bistros and trattorias of Ashland, but because I go to breakfast with my brother at the Main Street Café every time I go back to Missouri, I experienced no real culture shock.

That breakfast recalled a remark Tony Hillerman made when asked about his understanding of Navajos and their culture. He replied that he was basing his characterization in part on his experience of growing up in dirt-poor, Depression-ridden, rural Oklahoma, and country people of any race have a lot in common. So do people from small towns. Had my brother been with me, for example, he would have talked to half a dozen people about their families, jobs, and what was happening in Winston, just as I've seen him do in Hartford, Connecticut, and rural New Brunswick and everywhere else I've been with him.

There are other kinds of cultural crossovers. Once a Lakota student opened the door of my station wagon and said, "This is an *Indian* car!" Despite my cheekbones, I don't have any Indian blood that I know of, but it was true that the back seat and floor held a lot of stuff that I might need some day and wouldn't be useful anywhere else. Had she seen my brother's pickup, she would have sponsored him for adoption into the tribe. You can take the boy out of the country, but you can't get the junk out of his car.

One of the great things about the West is that many of us find it easy to move about and to be accepted. That was one of the things that enchanted Owen Wister in one of his early trips. He had been taken for an Englishman, a drummer, a bartender, and a stage driver, and he hated to go back east to a fixed identity.

But if the people are flexible, the popular perception of the myth of the West is not. Most Europeans and many Americans think of the West as telling one story, embodying one set of values, just as they think of all Indian cultures as essentially identical, and are puzzled, delighted, or resentful at having their views challenged.

Popular culture, from Ned Buntline to the latest Hollywood Western, is largely responsible for these misperceptions, partly because the reality is too complicated to represent dramatically. In *Warlock*, Oakley Hall attempted, with considerable success, to re-tell a version of the Tombstone story that deals not only with the townspeople-rustler rivalry but with conflicts between labor and management in the local mines and with the further confusion of military and civilian jurisdiction, with cross-border smuggling, and with the imaginative legacy of campaigns against the Apaches. The film adaptation was able to deal only with the mythic gunfighter and his opponents. And that was a good film.

And that's just in one town in one state. Any single myth of the West is a myth in the vulgar sense, not exactly a lie but not exactly not.

Anyway, each western state has its own myth, just as it has its own license plate and motto and state bird and tree and so on and on, and the differing myths are even more firmly fixed than the various flora and fauna designated by state legislators with nothing more important to do.

Even individual myths don't always cover the whole geographical territory, most notably in the states laid out with straightedges. Eastern Washington and Oregon have more in common with each other in landscape and economic development than either does with the territory west of the Cascades. The same thing is true, east-west, of Colorado and, north-south as well as east-west, of Arizona and New Mexico. Characters in Dan Jenkins's novel *Baja Oklahoma* discuss just how many distinct regions Texas can be divided into. Northern and southern California. And so on.

The Oklahoma to the north has two major myths. One is of people coming, whether in desperation or in hope. Indians in eastern Oklahoma remember, if not exactly celebrate, the dispossession from their homelands in what the Cherokees call the Trail of Tears and the Choctaws call the Long Sad Walk. And other nations have their own stories of dispossession. White Oklahomans celebrate 89er Day, the date of the first of several land runs, in which predominantly white people raced to stake claims on land conveniently not being used by the Indians. And then there is the submyth of the black towns—settled by former slaves and their descendants who had lit out for the territory in search of political freedom and economic self-determination.

The other myth, fixed by the novel and movie versions of *The Grapes of Wrath,* is of people leaving farms ruined in the dust bowl. Descendants of people who left Oklahoma acknowledge their origins cheerfully enough, but people in the state have taken a long time to get over the stigma attached to the term "Okie."

Kansas also has two myths. The oldest and most regionally confined is that of Bloody Kansas, where Free Soilers and Missouri guerillas battled in overtures to the Civil War. The other is that of trails—Kansas as a place to be traversed, not to go to. First was the

Santa Fe Trail, then the various routes for cattle drives up from Texas. Each confluence of trailhead and railhead had its own brief moment of notoriety, Dodge City being the last and most celebrated in popular culture.

Texas? The Alamo in the south, San Jacinto in the east. Comanches in the northwest. On the Llano Estacado, the two biggest post-conquest events were the invention of efficient windmills to draw water from the aquifer and the arrival of the railroad, which allowed settlers to build wooden houses.

Colorado? Might as well be Kansas up to the Front Range. After that, mining booms and busts. After that, ski resorts.

Oregon and Washington? Loggers from the mountains west; cattle, and not many of those, to the east, except where irrigation pumps have made the land fertile, like Yakima, which advertises itself as "The Palm Springs of Washington."

Arizona? Apache wars. A plethora of ghost towns. The Chamber of Commerce myth of the five C's: climate, citrus, copper, cattle, and cotton. But arable land is being bulldozed for housing developments, Phelps Dodge is losing money in its huge copper pits, and cattle are not making money either. In any case, none of these ever existed above the Mogollon Rim, and civic leaders are searching for new mottos and myths.

New Mexico? Depends on whom you consult: Hispanic, Anglo, Pueblo (and which pueblo, since neighbors for centuries can't stand each other), Navajo, Apache.

Utah? The Mormon trek westward and less heroic events like the Mountain Meadows Massacre. Polygamy, funny underwear, odd liquor laws. Buying the Winter Olympics with payments under the table.

Nevada outside Las Vegas and Reno? Who knows? California? Everyone is aware of its most obvious myths, but few know anything about northeast California, which might almost be a separate country.

No wonder that the West varies this much, for it is at least sixty percent as large as Europe in area; Texas is twenty-five percent larger than France, and both California and Montana are larger than Germany. And the landscape of the West has astonished Europeans for centuries.

Topography and hydrology are destiny anywhere in the world, but this is more obviously true in the West. East of the Rockies, one can go years at a time without thinking about geology. In the West, it is right in your face. Elevation, water resources, soil composition determine what kind of and how many people of any race could settle the land and be able to make a living from it. And that land can have a profound effect on the people: what they eat, almost everything they produce, how they vote, and how they look at the world.

For example, judging from their respective texts in the coffee-table books *Whatever the Wind Delivers: Celebrating West Texas and the Near Southwest* (Texas Tech, 1999) and *Fifty Miles from Home: Riding the Long Circle on a Nevada Family Ranch* (Nevada, 2002), Walt McDonald and Carolyn Dufurrena could undoubtedly sit down and talk about ranching and animals and problems with weather. But as the photographs in the two books show even more vividly than the texts, the two writers inhabit very different worlds. In Dufurrena's world, "Nevada looks like waves frozen in rock," while McDonald's Caprock is like an unruffled lake, though without any water and only telephone poles and windmills, and maybe a mesquite tree, vertical in the landscape.

McDonald is a fourth-generation West Texan who chopped cotton for "a thousand weeds a penny," envied the town boys who went to Roy Rogers movies, knew Buddy Holly, flew fighter jets in Vietnam, came back to find an uncle's ranch a shopping mall, does a little ranching on the side on what was meant to be cotton land if the Ogallala aquifer wasn't receding three feet a year. His work is hard but, judging from his poems, solitary, profitless, and more an act of family piety than an economic benefit or even necessity. Certainly it is not a legacy for his children and grandchildren, who have moved away from the land. His language, his aesthetic, and for that matter his metaphysical view are as simple and direct and as deceptively flat as the landscape of his poems. As if to underscore this viewpoint, the black and white photographs are taken from the archives of the Texas Tech Southwest Collection, not to present McDonald's world but to celebrate the departed pioneer past.

Dufurrena's world, presented in Linda Dufurrena's vivid color photographs, is still a working, family ranch in what the photographs show as a wildly varied landscape, and there will be another generation to work the ranch. There are threats: she speaks eloquently of the disappearance of family ranches as a result of purchase by government agencies, wealthy absentee owners, and corporate environmentalists. This, she concludes, breaks the covenant between the inhabitants and the land. But the polemic is muted, and the book concludes with six photographs, not of landscape stretching into the distance, but with medium shots of two generations of ropers, a sheepshearer, livestock, and finally the golden poplars at the ranch.

Both of these writers are working with variations on myths of the West—McDonald on the end of the West, popular since Frederick Jackson Turner, and Dufurrena on the Jeffersonian ideal of the self-sufficient farmer-rancher.

These myths are limiting, but they can also be enabling, as they are for McDonald and Dufurrena, who are adapting rather than replicating them. And it could be argued that westerners are lucky to have this kind of myth instead of the blandness of, say, Missouri history or the accumulated resentments of the Balkans or the Middle East or the Basques or Northern Irish. All people, individuals, families, and tribes, can be enriched by myth, but only if it is self-generated and self-sustained rather than imposed and if it can become a source of joy rather than anger and hatred.

Creating and transmitting myths—not lies or half-truths—is the job of writers and storytellers who are in touch with their peoples, their family and broader cultural heritage, and the land and history that helped to shape them. Any story, as long as it is not constricted by generic formulae or the pieties of official history, can be part of a saga, and from saga it is a short step to authentic myth. And perhaps a longer step to a coherent vision of one's world that can be shared with others and help to shape their worlds.